BROAD

A VILLAGE HISTORY

by Derek Parsons

To: Mike 'Archie' Ologist - Rees

From: G. O'Fizz (the Irish lemonade bottle)

THE CORNMILL PRESS

Published by The Cornmill Press, 11 Cornmill Close, Elmley Castle, Pershore, Worcestershire, WR10 3JH

1996 (Reprinted 2001)

© Copyright Derek Parsons
All rights reserved

No part of this publication may be reproduced or transmitted in any form or by any means without prior written permission of the publisher.

ISBN 0 9527904 0 8

****

Printed by Vale Press Ltd, 6 Willersey Business Park, Willersey, Broadway, Worcestershire. WR12 7RR
Tel: 01386 858900 Fax: 01386 858475

Title Page: Example of Bronze brooch found in Anglo-Saxon cemetery on Broadway Hill
    (Courtesy: Society of Antiquaries)

CONTENTS

Chapter One: **Domesday and Before**
Origin of name, Evidence of Iron-Age & Roman occupation, Anglo-Saxon cemetery, Grant of Manor to Pershore Abbey, 972 Charter, Domesday Survey.

Chapter Two: **Highways and Byways**
Ancient boundaries and trackways, Development of the High Street, The Upend and Nether End, The Manor House and 'Bradeweye's Greate Farm,' The Common fields and Village Green.

Chapter Three: **The 'Towneship' of Broadway**
Award of Borough privilege, The Manor Courts, Lay Subsidy Roll, The Black Death, Growth in population, Coaching era, Enclosure

Chapter Four: **Church and Religion**
Church buildings, Religious difficulties, Bishop's visits, Quakers, The Drunken Parson, Rise of Non-conformism, Trouble at the Vicarage

Chapter Five: **Markets, Fairs and Recreations**
13th century Grant of market and fair, Wool Trade, Whitsun celebrations, Games and other pastimes, Jubilees and other celebrations

Chapter Six: **Law, War and Disturbance**
Broadway's first criminal, Battle of the Fishponds, English Civil War, King Charles' visit, Broadway Plot, Parish Constable, Public whippings, Mr. Wynniatt's murder, Attempted assassination of Tax Collectors, Political agitation

Chapter Seven: **Custom, Folklore and Superstition**
Ancient customs, Oak-Apple Day, Charitable giving, Bells of St. Eadburghas, Broadway's Ghosts, Fish Hill, Murder of Joseph Dyer, Burglary at Madame Harpur's.

Chapter Eight: **The Jewel of the Cotswolds**
The 'Discovery' of Broadway, Economic revival, The Fire Brigade, The changing nature of village life.

NOTE TO SECOND EDITION

Since this history was published five years ago, Broadway has witnessed several important changes. Most notably, the long-awaited by-pass has finally been built; some thirty years after it was first mooted. As a consequence, the upper High Street has been controversially closed to through traffic.

Broadway has also lost its largest employer with the closure of the Gordon Russell furniture factory. This loss is especially personal, as it was where I spent much of my early working life. The four-acre factory site, in the heart of the village, is due to be redeveloped as housing. The scheme is also intended to include a Heritage Centre and a Tourist Information office; a recognition of the importance of Broadway's past, and of tourism to the Village's future.

Otherwise, little else has changed and I have not thought it necessary, at the moment, to revise my narrative. As before, I would like to thank the following people and organizations who helped me during the preparation of this book: the staff of the Evesham and Worcester Libraries, and of the Worcester County Record Offices; Chris Sealy who read the manuscript and made helpful suggestions; the staff of Birmingham Reference Library; Geoff Dyer and John Parsons for help with the photographic content, Roland and Heather Jones for the use of their facilities, and the many others who offered advice and assistance. I would also like to express my gratitude to those who gave permission to reproduce illustrations and photographs. Finally, I must thank my parents for their support, and my brother, Brian, for his excellent photographic work and invariably sound advice.

Derek Parsons 25 Sept. 2001

FOREWORD

Broadway is an ancient settlement whose origins are lost in the mists of time. By the Eleventh Century, however, the village was already well-established, and apparently thriving. It continued to prosper, becoming a borough by the thirteenth. The following two centuries saw it decline somewhat in the wake of the Black Death. Its fortunes were then revived during the late sixteenth century after the Reformation relieved Pershore Abbey of ownership. There followed three centuries of almost unbroken growth, during which the population increased to something like five times its Elizabethan level. At this time the village became a great coaching centre. But the introduction of rail in Britain during the 1840's reduced the passing trade on which Broadway relied, and the village then settled down into a very quiet place, the haunt of artists and the like. The arrival of the motor car at the turn of the 20th century, and the advent of tourism, restored Broadway's vitality, placing it now among the most frequently visited of all Cotswold villages. This, in brief, is Broadway's history. But what of the detail?

O, call back yesterday, bid time return.

(Shakespeare)

CHAPTER ONE

DOMESDAY AND BEFORE

Broadway nestles at the foot of the Cotswold Hills, at the very southern tip of Worcestershire in the wide and fertile Vale of Evesham. Owning no special place in history, - its repute lies in its famed natural beauty, - it nevertheless has a rich, and occasionally colourful, past which stretches back to the Dark Ages and beyond. The village is said to derive its name from the broad natural sweep of the landscape, which falls steeply away from the Cotswold escarpment into Evesham Vale, and not, as one might suppose, from the broad High Street which today is one of its most admired features. A 9th century source refers to Broadway as Bradsetena Gamere, or 'broad village,' whilst later documents, which range from the Anglo-Saxon through Old English to Modern English, style it variously Bradanuuege (10th c.), Bradweia (11th c.), and Bradway or Bradeweye (13th c. and later). The modern spelling and pronunciation 'Broadway' seems to date from the late 16th century, when the High Street itself was known as 'The Broadway', although 'Bradway' remained in common usage until the 18th century.

Opinions differ about when the land was first settled. Traces of occupation dating from the later Roman period (3rd and 4th century) have been found in the lower village near the football ground, indicating a semi-permanent settlement covering some ten acres. Coins from the reign of Tiberius, Roman Emperor at the time of Christ, discovered at Middle Hill during work on foundations, hint at a contemporary or slightly earlier settlement on the southern slopes. Scattered remains dating from the Stone-Age and Iron-Age periods, unearthed in parts of the lower village, point to the transient presence of Ancient Britons. Of greater significance, perhaps, are the reputed remains of an ancient long barrow, and Iron-Age hillfort, which lie beneath the turf of Broadway Golf Course, suggesting that the

A picture postcard view of Broadway and the Vale of Evesham, C. 1930

escarpment, which forms a natural defensive position, was anciently employed as a vantage point from which to defend against potential marauders.

An important archeological discovery of recent years was the unearthing of an Anglo-Saxon cemetery during quarrying work in 1954. Situated further along the escarpment, between the entrance to Tower Drive and Broadway Tower, and about one hundred and fifty metres from the road on the Broadway side, the cemetery was found to contain eight graves dating from the early sixth century. The skeletal remains, as far as identification allowed, were those of three females, two given as aged between twenty and thirty and a slightly older woman, and three males of a broadly similar age range. The men were described as of muscular build. Knives, spears, beads, decorative brooches and silver rings, found with the bodies, suggest they were members of a well-to-do, though not wealthy group. Their settlement is assumed to have been located on the brow of the hill, within easy reach of the burial ground. Three ancient trackways pass nearby, the Great White Way, a prehistoric salt road; Buckle Street, also believed to be prehistoric; and Ryknild Street, a Roman road.

It is probable that Broadway once contained a number of settlements such as that indicated by the presence of the Anglo-Saxon cemetery. These may well have comprised extended family groups living and farming independently of their neighbours, though trading produce and intermarrying. A village centred on the High Street was most likely a later development, and may date from the 7th or 8th century, a period of widespread agrarian reforms. It is known that in 577 the 'Hwicce', a warrior tribe of West Saxons, swept into the region subduing the local Celts and ultimately settling themselves on the land. Several decades later another Saxon tribe, the Mercians, established themselves as overlords of a vast area known as Mercia which included the kingdom of Hwicce, of which Worcestershire was by then a part. In the 650's, following the death of Penda, the heathen king of Mercia, the Mercians adopted Christianity, and about the year 679, as a result of Archbishop Theodore's work, the kingdom of Hwicce became the new Diocese of Worcester. At this point, the population of England (although the name was not yet current) began to increase. In order to feed the people vast tracts of land were cleared and put under cultivation. The concept of common land was introduced, and the practice of farming large open fields on a two or three year rotation was adopted. The exceptional fertility of the soil in the Evesham Vale, and the plentiful supply of natural springs and streams, when coupled with the excellent pasture land of the hill slopes, must have placed Broadway among the more favoured sites.

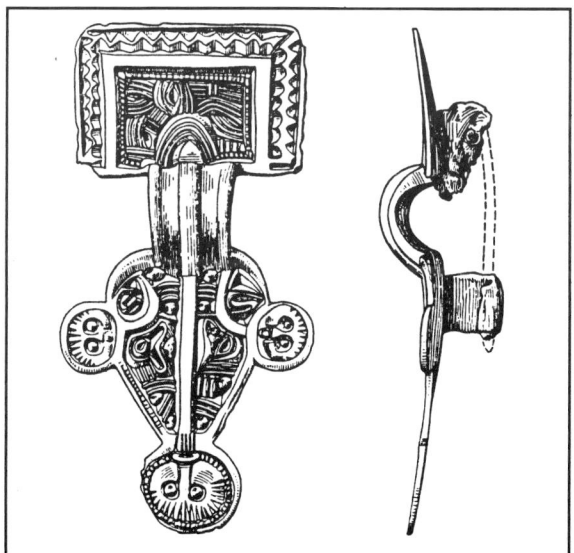

Bronze brooch found in Anglo-Saxon cemetery, Broadway Hill.
(Courtesy: Society of Antiquaries)

This postcard from the early days of tourism, circa 1890, shows the broad High Street for which Broadway is famous.

From the 7th century, Christianity became firmly established in the lives of Anglo-Saxon tribesmen and women. To atone for their often barbarian pasts, successive kings and overlords embraced the new religion, promoting the foundation of religious houses which they endowed with generous grants of land. By the 11th century more than one third of the nation's land was in church hands, a situation that remained unchallenged until the wholesale seizure of church property by King Henry VIII in the 16th century.

Pershore Abbey, whose history is inextricably linked with that of Broadway, is a case in point. Leland describes the monastery as originating around 689, and attributes this to Oswald, a nephew of Ethelred, King of the Mercians. Initially the Abbey is thought to have operated on secular principles. Following the Council of Clovesho in 747, Benedictine tenets were probably introduced, although it is unlikely the rules of St. Benedict, namely poverty, chastity and obedience, were followed in any meaningful sense. Ultimately the Abbey suffered the fate of so many of our religious houses, and was dissolved by the Crown in 1539. Today only a fragment of the original Abbey complex survives.

The 8th and 9th centuries were characterised by frequent invasions of the Danes or 'Northmen.' Sporadic action against the overlords of Wessex,

St, Eadburgha's, the late 12th century Norman church in the Bury End which is thought to have replaced a previous Saxon church. (Photo: B. Parsons)

Mercia, Northumbria and the lesser kingdoms greatly disrupted the economy, invaders wreaking destruction on the countryside. Peace was restored, for a time, in 955 under King Edred, and in 959 his nephew, known aptly as Edgar the Peaceable was proclaimed king. Under the influence of Archbishop Dunstan of Canterbury, many religious and political reforms were undertaken. Edgar is credited with instituting the Ordinance of the Hundred, by which shires were divided into smaller districts called Hundreds, the inhabitants being made responsible for the suppression of robbery, murder and violence in their respective districts. Broadway became part of Pershore Hundred. Major reforms were also undertaken in the monasteries. Benedictine rules were reintroduced where they had lapsed, and more strictly enforced where fallen into decay. The reward for those willing to comply with church edicts was the grant or restoration of land for the support of their houses, the details of which were set down in a great charter dated 972. Included is a description of land of the Manor of Broadway granted to the Benedictine monks at Pershore Abbey.

Edgar's charter recites that the King is pleased to grant to the convent at Pershore, dedicated to the ever blessed Virgin Mary and apostles Peter and

Paul, all the privileges bestowed on them by his predecessor Coenulf (possibly Coenwulf King of Mercia who died 821) at the request of Duke Beornoth, together with the liberty of electing a head according to the rule of St. Benedict after the death of the then abbot, Foldbriht, 'in whose time this liberty has been restored.' This last remark implies that Benedictine rules were not simply being introduced but reinstated, as were the privileges once accorded the monks. Whether these former privileges included ownership of Broadway Manor remains unclear. We therefore cannot be certain who owned the manor prior to 972. However, it is possible that Pershore Abbey had held Broadway from the time of its foundation, circa 689. An earlier charter records that Evesham monastery, founded in 703, held the surrounding manors of Badsey, Willersey, Childswickham, Honeybourne and Bretforton, there being no mention of Broadway. As Pershore was situated on an ancient trackway, which linked South Wales and London, the route of which passed through Broadway, clearly it would have been an attractive manor for the Abbey to hold.

The monks were not allowed the quiet enjoyment of their charter lands for long. King Edgar died in 975 and this signalled a sudden and unexpected reign of terror. The agent of that terror, a truly black-hearted villain, was Duke Alphere, Earldorman of Mercia who, as a signatory to the Charter, had tacitly approved the re-establishment of the benedictine monasteries. Freed from the King's influence he began instead 'by rapine and pillage' to sack the religious houses of his Earldom. Feeding on local resentment against the clergy, he cleared many of its monasteries and convents, appropriating their land and property, and installing his followers, thus accruing to himself the rents, tithes, customary fines and other benefits of the holdings. Pershore Abbey, like that of Evesham, was sacked in 976 and the monks ejected. Alphere's plundering ended abruptly in 983 when he died, so it is said, 'eaten of vermin.' Abbot Foldbriht was reinstated at Pershore and died in 988. Alphere's son, Odda, then made restitution for the lands and property sequestered by his father, and grandly vowed a vow of perpetual virginity, lest his offspring be given to similar crimes. He adopted the habit of a monk at Deerhurst and after his death in 1056 was carried to Pershore Abbey for burial.

Duke Alphere's plundering was one of many troubles to beset the monks of Pershore during the 10th and 11th centuries. In 1002, the year King Elthelred ordered the massacre of all Danes living in England, the Abbey was destroyed by fire. It was rebuilt, and reconsecrated in 1020. Edward the Confessor (reigned 1042-1066), then gifted the majority of its charter lands to the Abbey of Westminster which became, at this time, one of the richest

Domesday and Before

Wickham Hill, looking towards Childswickham. This marks one of the earliest known boundaries between the two villages, being recorded in an 8th century charter.
(Photo: B. Parsons)

in England. Broadway was among a handful of manors Pershore Abbey was allowed to retain for its support.

The death of Edward the Confessor in 1066 precipitated that momentous event, the Norman Conquest. Twenty years later the Normans commissioned a survey to record every man living in the Kingdom, his status and possessions. This task was accomplished with typical Norman thoroughness, as Florence of Worcester, a monk and contemporary chronicler dryly remarked:

"King William caused all England to be surveyed; how much each of his barons possessed; and how many enfeoffed knights; and how many ploughs, villeins, animals and livestock each one possessed in all his kingdom from the greatest to the least; and what dues each estate was able to render. And as a consequence the land was vexed with much violence."

The Survey provides our first glimpse into village life. The entry for Broadway is brief, but instructive. In translation it reads:

Domesday and Before

Land of St. Mary's at Pershore

The Church holds Bradweia itself. Thirty hides which pay tax. In Lordship three ploughs. A priest and forty-two villeins with twenty ploughs. Eight serfs. Value of the whole before 1066 £12.10s, now £14.10s. A free man held two and a half hides of this land before 1066. He bought them from Abbot Edmund (of Pershore). The land was part of the lordship land. Now two ploughs in the Abbot's lordship for his supplies. The value was, and is, 30s. Urso claims back this land as the King's gift. He states he exchanged it himself with the Abbot for one Manor which was part of his lordship.

At thirty hides, or some three and a half thousand acres, Broadway was the largest of Pershore Abbey's scattered holdings, representing one quarter of its assets in terms of acreage and income. As Domesday indicates, the manor's value had increased by one sixth since King Edward's reign, suggesting it was little affected by the Conquest. The great disruption to the economy caused by the Conquest was felt more in the north, where the refusal to submit to Norman rule led to vast areas being laid waste for generations. However, Broadway was untypical even of Worcestershire manors where average values fell by about a quarter. This points to some resilience in the local economy.

As only male heads of households were recorded in the survey, one must multiply by a factor of about five to determine the population. Broadway's entry therefore suggests a Domesday village of about two hundred and twenty souls. The priest and serfs are assumed to be unmarried. This indicates that Broadway was, in medieval terms at least, a substantial village, of which two hundred inhabitants were members of the villein class, bonded peasants who paid labour service to the lord in return for strips in the common fields, and the remainder 'servi' or slaves, chattels of their lord who could be bought and sold in the same manner as animals and produce. The proportion of the two classes at Broadway appears typical of West Midland manors. We can therefore characterise 11th century Broadway as a well-established, and apparently thriving feudal community. One where none of its inhabitants was free, but where some had more liberty than others, - its 'servi' perhaps decendants of the original Celtic tribes, enslaved after some long-forgotten battle.

CHAPTER TWO

HIGHWAYS AND BYWAYS

Broadway's boundaries are clearly very ancient, but for the most part their origin remains obscure. King Edgar's charter contains the earliest known description, which indicates that the 10th century boundaries corresponded closely to the present parish limits. Curiously, the boundary clause contained in the charter embraces the neighbouring manor of Childswickham. Why this might be is unclear, although several later documents suggest the two were linked. Peasants are known to have shared 'Rights of Common' on certain lands abutting the boundary. There are several translations of the Anglo-Saxon script. A recent interpretation is contained within 'Worcestershire Anglo-Saxon Charter Boundaries' by Della Hooke. It reads (in italics):

'First from the boundary end to Pease Brook,' The Pease Brook, a small stream which passes through the West End of the village, is the name of an existing farm on the Cheltenham Road. *'Thence to the headlands at west meadow,'* This lies in the far north-western corner of the parish. *'From west meadow to the headlands,'* arable land lying in Childswickham parish. *'So that to thistle mere,'* a place within Childswickham Manor recorded in an 8th century charter. *'From the mere along the slade valley to pincan dene,'* pincan dene or finches valley is also recorded in the earlier charter. *'From the finches valley so that up to the top of the hill of the thorns, thence to the post.'* This was probably a finger post situated on the Childswickham to Hinton-on-the-Green road at Mount Pleasant. The Childswickham boundary crosses at a right-angle to the road at this point. *'From the post over the old cleared land so that to fugel (bird) low.'* *'From the low to Egsa's marsh, from the marsh up along the hill.'* *'So that to Baedda's spring,'* (Badsey Brook). At this point we rejoin the Broadway boundary. *'From Baedda's*

Highways and Byways

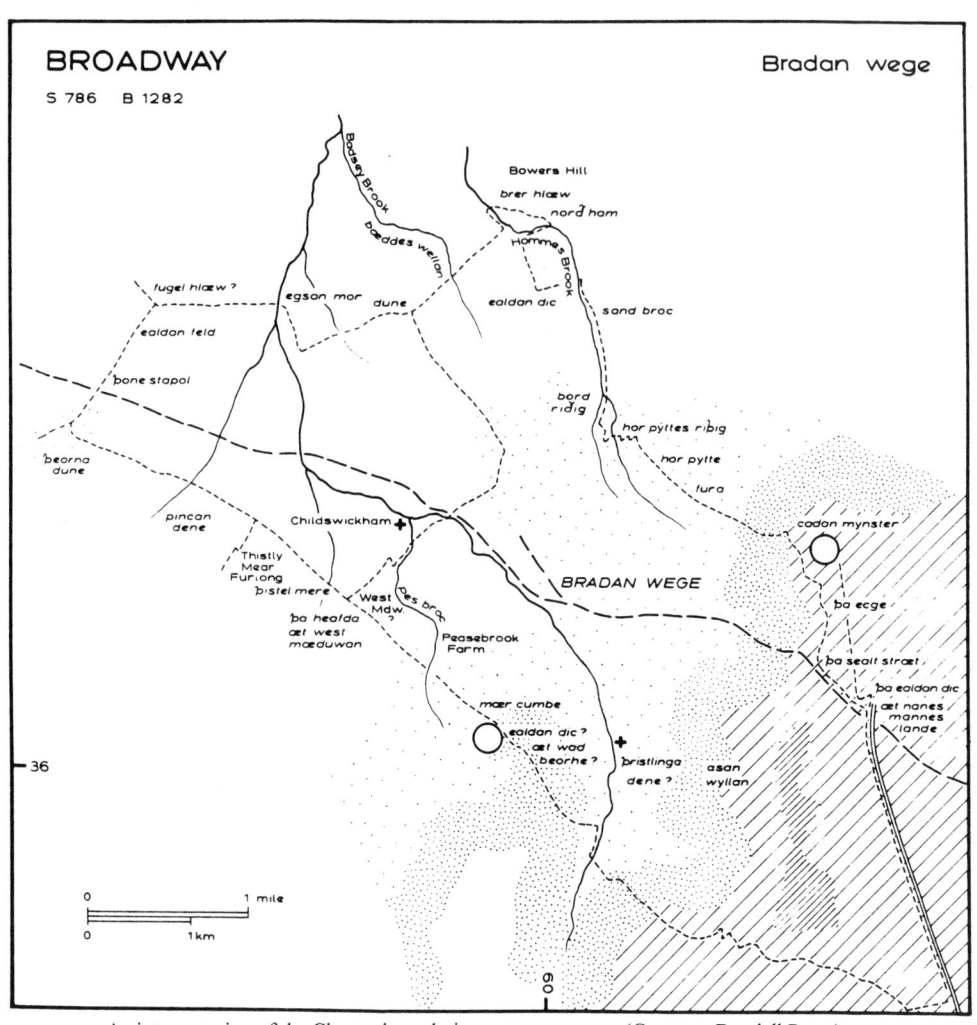

An interpretation of the Charter boundaries. (Courtesy Boydell Press)

spring to briar low,' (Bowers Hill), *from the low to the north watermeadow, around the meadow along the old dyke, so that to Sand Brook.' 'From Sand Brook to the plank? streamlet, thence to the streamlet of the dirty pit.'* We are now situated in the hollow near the old railway bridge in Collin Lane. *'From the dirty pit along the furrow so that to Cada's minster.'* Here the boundary follows the escarpment, passing in front of Foxhill Manor and behind Farncombe House. Cada's minster, which apparently stood on, or adjacent to, the present golf course, was possibly an ancient 'Mother Church' serving several of the surrounding manors, although no evidence of the building has yet come to light. The suggestion is of a christianised pagan shrine. *'Thence to the edge,'* following the escarpment, *'so that to the salt street'*, a small stretch of the Great White Way, one of many ancient saltways which traversed the kingdom. *'Along the street to the old dyke at nanes mannes lande,'* (No-Man's Land). This small patch of waste ground, located just beyond the picnic area at the top of Fish Hill on the Worcestershire/ Gloucestershire border, is recorded in an 18th century application for a toll-road. *'From the dyke to Asa's spring.'* We are now on the south-eastern escarpment of the village. *'From Asa's spring to the bold? persons valley.'* This lies in the hollow beyond St.Eadburgha's church. It is suggested the name refers to the presence of local bandits. in what was probably then a heavily wooded area. However, another source translates the Anglo-Saxon script as 'Thistle' valley. *'From the valley upwards so that to the old dyke at woad barrow, along the dyke again to the boundary coomb.'* This completes the circuit of Broadway and Childswickham Manors. The missing boundary between Broadway and Childswickham can be inferred from the 8th century Childswickham charter. As indicated by the map, from the West meadow near Peasebrook, it travels northwards passing

A rare example of a cruck framed house, Bury End, of a type that would have been common in medieval days. (Photo: B. Parsons)

up Wickham Hill by Pennylands, and continues in a westerly direction towards the parish of Wickhamford, running parallel for some distance with the ridgeway road to Evesham.

Broadway's roads, footpaths and bridleways were established over many centuries in response to the changing needs of the village, and do not easily lend themselves to analysis. Occasionally, however, it is possible to spot where an ancient field boundary has developed into a more permanent track. Springfield Lane is an example, marking the boundary between the Sand and the Rudgeway, two of Broadway's great pre-enclosure fields. The Leamington Road to Willersey is known to follow, for a good part of its length, the upper boundary between the Sand and Shearfield.

Until the early part of the last century, traffic entering the village from Pershore did so by way of Pry Lane, passing along West End Lane and turning left at Pie Corner to enter the village via the Snowshill Road. It has been suggested that originally traffic turned right at Pie Corner and surmounted the hill by way of the Conigree Lane which lies opposite the old church of St. Eadburgha's. An ancient footpath, which leads to Dor Knapp and Middle Hill, exits close to Broadway Tower. It is probable, however, that by the early Medieval period, and perhaps for a considerable age before, there existed a permanent track leading from the upper High Street to the summit, carrying traffic through, what was by the 13th century, a market town.

We can be fairly certain the High Street had become the centre of habitation by the 11th century. There have been regrettably few opportunities for archeological investigation of the area. But the presence of some fifty households at the time of Domesday, and the lack of evidence from other, more accessible, areas of the manor of any sizable settlement, strongly supports this argument. The High Street afforded convenient access to the common fields on the northern (Lygon Arms) side of the manor, and was serviced by two streams fed by springs rising on the hill. These ran the length of the street, joining at the bottom near the village green, and provided that essential supply of fresh water. The early inhabitants built their rough timber-framed hovels on the far side of these streams, thus creating the broad street that is so characteristic of the village. Behind their houses they enclosed small parcels of land for gardens, or 'Greensward.' On the northern side of the High Street these extended to the Back Lane.

At some, as yet, undiscovered date, the Manor was apparently divided into two parts. These are described in early documents as the Uppey or Upend, and the West or Nether End. The Uppey End contained the High Street and

The Court, Bury End, pictured here around 1820, was the Gatehouse to the long defunct Manor House which stood in fields opposite.

the common fields and wastes for the support of the peasantry on the northern side of the village, whilst the Nether End mainly comprised the demesne lands of the lordship. The demesne lands included the rich pasture of the southern slopes. A section of the boundary between the Upend and Nether End was marked by the Stonehill Brook and the lower reaches of the Mill Brook with which it joins below the Waterloo Bridge on the Snowshill road. The Manor House of the village lay squarely within the demesne lands in a field opposite St. Eadburgha's church. It was here that the Lord of the Manor (originally the Abbot of Pershore) transacted business and held court, reference being made in 1760 for a tenant *'to keep one bay at the North End in repair called the Courthouse.'* The house was demolished in 1773, and probably gives Bury End its name. In Old English, the word burg or byrig means a fortified place, manor or house. Records of the Manor Court rolls dating from the 14th century refer to *'Le Bury Stret,'* which one can conceivably identify as the present Snowshill Road. Thus 'The Bury Street' led from the main village to 'the byrig' or Manor House at the 'byrig end' of the village.

The Manor House of the village was attached to several thousand acres known as *'Bradweye's Greate Farm,'* a detailed description of which is contained in a lease dated 1618. Owned until the Reformation by the monks of Pershore the estate was purchased in 1558 by William Babington, whose

The Upper High Street, about 1930.

grandson, Sir William, sold it to the sitting tenant Anne Daston, widow of Anthony Daston of Dumbleton. Anne, in turn, settled the property on Walter and Anthony Savage, sons from a previous marriage to Francis Savage of Elmley Castle. Anthony died in 1587 and his son John inherited, whilst Anne herself died at the Manor House in 1619 aged about 91. Habington the Elizabethan historian, having once spent an enjoyable sojourn at the house, grandly described Anne as *'the most bountiful gentlewoman for hospitality of her degree in England.'* Around 1620 Walter and John sold land to Sir Thomas (later Lord) Coventry, whose family seat was at Croome in Worcestershire. A later Lord Coventry built the unusual three-turreted tower at the top of Fish Hill. The Manor House and Middle Hill estate remained in the Savage family until the death of George Savage in 1793. The will of Mary Savage (d.1658), the widow of Walter Savage (d.1640), contains an inventory of belongings discovered in the house and outbuildings. Among a number of mundane items are listed three hundred and twenty fleeces and forty bushels of fruit, evidence of large scale sheep farming and of the great orchards which lay adjacent to the Manor House. In the yard was found some wood and 'four tons of coal,' the latter a rather unexpected discovery given the absence of a local supply.

Fourteenth century rolls of the Broadway Manor Court make frequent mention of *'Le Portstreet,'* which one can speculate was the medieval name

Highways and Byways

A Rural Scene. The Village Green about 1905

of the High Street. The name suggests the presence of a Portmote court. The obscure term *'Wennebrugg'* or *'Winnebrugg,'* also appears frequently in medieval records, and seemingly refers to a bridge. There are very few in Broadway, although doubtless one of some importance once existed near Pie Corner where the main West End entrance to the village crossed the Mill Brook. *Stauntons Lane,* recorded in a document dated 1379, may be part of the present Cotswold Way. This track crosses West End Lane passing through Broadway Coppice, on its way to Stanton and beyond. Conigree Lane, reputedly one of the oldest trackways in the village, is not mentioned in very early records, although a *Warners* (Warrener's) *Lane* is found. The likelihood is that both refer to the same lane opposite St. Eadburgha's. A Subsidy Roll dating from about 1280 refers to a *'Warnerio,'* who was presumably the Lord of the Manor's warrener, the husbanding of rabbits being an important activity.

A few of Broadway's field names give a clue to their origin and use, although the meaning of many still remains delightfully obscure. On the southern side of the village, Deanes Meadow, once attached to the Manor House, is thought to be named from the Dean of Campden, to whom the Abbot of Pershore was obliged to report. Others recorded during the 16th and 17th centuries include Kings Gaston, the Over and Nether Willyssides, the Foregrove, the Langett and Great and Little Bearfurlong, (later described as Great and Little Conygree). Among those fields whose location is definitely known are, The Dorton (presumably Darton fields opposite the houses in Cheltenham Road), Middle Hill and Seven Wells, two names that have apparently remained unchanged for at least four centuries.

The common fields of the Upper End appear generally to be named from aspects of their geography. Below Farncombe on the northern slope is found the Lynches. As its name indicates it was once a terraced piece of farmland. Adjacent to it is Green Street, a field that covers some ten acres. The name is first recorded in the 14th century, and its designation as a street suggests it was used as a thoroughfare linking the common arable fields of the lower slopes with the hill pasture around Farncombe. Below Green Street is the peculiarly named Mitchbratch, and joined to its northern border is the equally obscurely named Bibsworth. Mitchbratch perhaps means 'much broken' implying the field had an arable use. Moving further down, parallel to the High Street on the northern side, we reach Shearfield, once one of the great open arable field. This has been much built upon during the present century. Adjoining it is the Sands, which derives its name from the sandy nature of the soil. This too has seen housing development in recent years. To the north of the Sands, the land rises through Horseway to Great and

Little Collin, the latter fields presumably deriving their names from the Norman French 'col' meaning small hill. To the west of the Sands is the Rudgeway (or ridgeway), which contains the houses of Station Road. In the lower village, at the bottom of the Childswickham Road, we find Ham Meadow and Ham Furlong, 'ham' referring to land lying adjacent to a stream, the Mill Brook. This was once common land, where villagers grew winter feed for cattle and oxen.

The village Green is found, as one might expect, at the heart of the village, at the junction of the High Street and Snowshill Road. It was here that anciently markets, fairs, and other informal diversions, took place. Its history is poorly documented, though it is presumed to have existed from earliest times. An oblique reference can be found in a 13th century tax assessment, known as a Subsidy Roll, where a William de la Grene appears. A Gregory atte Grene is mentioned in a slightly later roll. Originally more extensive than at present, it once included the car park area below the Swan Inn. Road widening and paving naturally reduced its scope, until today the area it occupies is quite modest. We must, however, be grateful that representations made to the Parish Council in the 1920's that it be laid to tarmac to accommodate the burgeoning tourist traffic, were not adopted.

CHAPTER THREE

THE 'TOWNESHIP' OF BROADWAY

The early medieval period was recognisably a time of growth and prosperity for Broadway, and at some point during the 13th century this culminated in the award of Borough status. The privileges gained from such awards varied from borough to borough, but the common element was the much coveted burgage tenure, (the alienation of mortmain) which freed the burgesses of the borough from the customary duties of manorialism, enabling them to pay a money rent for their land, as well as allowing them to sell and bequeath their properties freely. The award also presupposed freeman status on the part of the burgesses. For Broadway this marked a considerable departure from the entirely peasant community that had existed just two centuries earlier. An example of this new found independence is the transfer in 1213 of two virgates (sixty acres) of land in Broadway, between Roger of Broadway and Matilda of Cirencester, without the intercession of the Abbot.

The earliest surviving records of the Broadway borough court date from 1379. These indicate that the burgages (the houses and their associated land) had, in the recent past, been held by a governing body at Broadway, to which was paid the rents and customary fines such as the 'heriot,' - the forfeit of the family's best animal on the death of the householder. However, it appears that by the late 14th century the one shilling rent, (known as port rent), was rendered directly to the Abbot of Pershore as Lord of the Manor, by the hand of the port-bailiff every three weeks at the lord's court at Broadway. This suggests there had occurred a significant decline in the power of the burgesses.

The Manor Courts, (latterly those of the Courts Leet and Baron), originally sat at the Manor House in the Bury End. But after the Dissolution

Broadway High Street and the Lygon Arms Hotel. A scene from about 1920.

of Pershore Abbey in the 16th century, the Manor House became a purely private residence, and they were commonly held instead in a chapel that previously stood on the site occupied today by St. Michael's church. Here the men of the village would gather each October to elect officers of the court for the coming year, and make such new orders governing the use of common land as they thought fit. If the weather allowed, the court met outdoors, as it did in 1697 in a field called Football Close. In December the officers would meet again to *'decide controversies'* and impose fines for breaches of orders that had occurred during the year. Typical complaints included allowing pigs into the fields unringed, (thus damaging the land), and fouling the brook. An instruction of the Court Leet dated 1711 dictated that *'no person shall empty any Chamber Potts, Soape Sudds or Bucking Lye* (an alkaline solution used for washing clothes) *or suffer any mixen to run into the Common Streame on payne of 10s each default.'*

When the surviving court rolls begin in 1379, the officers of the borough comprise the two bailiffs of the portmote court, (or portreeves), the tithingmen of the Upend and Westend, (respectively two and one), two ale-tasters, and two overseers of flesh, or *'cadaveratores'*, assisted by a jury of twelve men. The presence of two sets of tithingmen underlines the geographical division to which we have already referred, and indicates that by the 14th century a majority of villagers inhabited the Upend, or High

Elizabethan cottages in the Upper High Street (Photo: B.Parsons)

Street area, thus necessitating twice as many officers to undertake collection of the tithes.

In ceding the routine governance of village affairs to burgesses, by granting borough status, the Abbey had not merely deputised responsibility for local affairs, it had surrendered many valuable customary rights. However, its control over manor affairs was not entirely lost. Where not enshrined by charter, and none is known to exist for Broadway, it was possible for privileges to be removed, even for borough status to be revoked. Successive abbots, it is clear, did not allow free reign at Broadway. Court rolls indicate that borough courts were usually held by the steward of the Abbot, who doubtless ensured his master's interests were fully represented. Ordinances of the court were made by the steward at the *request* or with the *consent* of the tenants. In the event, borough status effectively lapsed during the long decline that followed the Black Death. Whilst references are still found to the 'Town' of Broadway as late as the 18th century, it no longer operated as a borough, and had not done so for many generations.

The early medieval period marked the gradual decline of serfdom, and the substitution of customary duties for cash payment. The period also witnessed the rapid growth and diversification of the economy. The 'servi' or slave class (of which Broadway had eight members in 1086) had all but disappeared by 1200, absorbed into the more numerous villein class. Specialisation of labour in return for money wages became an increasing feature, and we discover among contemporary records a new breed of artisan whose livelihood was not derived solely from the land. Even so, subsistence farming remained the principal means by which the majority kept body and soul together.

A Lay Subsidy Roll of circa 1280 illustrates some of these changes. The roll is a unique survivor from the 13th century and exists only for Worcestershire. The entry for Broadway contains a list of taxpayers and amounts paid.

De Abbate de Persor 5 marks (£3.6s.8d)

De Willielmo Palmar 3/-	De Warnerio 2/6d
De Alexandro Juvene 3/-	De Willielmo filio Juliane 2/6d
De Thoma Preposito 2/-	De Roberto Marmyun 6/-
De Willielmo Stampeto 1/6d	De Ricardo Dolent 1/-
De Johanne Marmyun 7/4d	De Johanne Cainham 4/10d
De Alicia relicta Johannis Clarice 6/-	De Margeria relicta Rogeri Prepositi 3/-
	De Willielmo Egade 3/6d
De Ricardo Gyrre 2/6d	De Willielmo le Smale 3/-
De Jordano le Horsmon 6/-	De Henrico Nichol' 2/-
De Ricardo le Newemon 4/-	De Willielmo de la Grene 3/8d
De Johanne le Horsmon	De Johanne de Draycote 10/-
De Alicia la Palmare 4/-	De Roberto filio Prepositi 3/-
De Roberto de Clere 7/-	De Roberto de Estenovere 4/8d
De Willielmo Gilb' 4/10d	De Hugone Molendinario 3/-
De Adam de Mathine 18/-	De Ricardo Fabro 2/6d
De Philippo Capellano 15/-	De Cristina la Quarreur 1/-
De Ricardo de Fraxino 8/-	De Cristina relicta Rogeri Bercarii 1/8d
De Johanne Folyot 4/6d	De Rogero Ede 1/-
De Willelmo de Cleydon 3/6d	De Alexandro Alecoc 3/-
De Willielmo Thurstein 1/8d	De Simone Molendinario 1/4d
De Roberto filio Johannis 7/-	De Galfrido de Lutlinton 1/-
De Roberto Thursteyn 6/-	De Rogero Agace 4/-
De Johanne Hogemon 6/-	De Willielmo le Somenur 1/8d.
De Anna relicta Johannis 1/8d	
De Johanne de Northclyve 6/-	
De Nicholao Marmyun 6/6d	Summa £14.2s.2d
De Willielmo Fabro 2/6d	
De Willielmo del Overe 2/6d	********
De Waltero le Skay 1/8d	
De Rogero Gilb' 4/-	

Lechmere Roll 1275-1280 (Transcribed: E. Howard)

The table is useful in permitting us to estimate the 13th century population of Broadway. Fifty two villagers, or heads of households, are listed as rendering tax. To that number must be added those who, for one reason or another, do not appear on the roll; those who had undertaken military service to the King and were thus exempt, or had paid scutage in lieu of service, as well as many simply too poor to pay, for example servants and landless labourers. After allowing for this missing underclass we might reasonably suppose a population of between four and six hundred. Broadway would therefore have been, in medieval terms, a settlement of some significance. Indeed, the county town of Worcester, by comparison, had only six times as many registered taxpayers, whilst Evesham, seemingly the second most populous town in the county, had only about twice Broadway's number.

The largest taxpayer at Broadway, other than the Abbot of Pershore, was Adam de Mathine, whose surname indicates that he was 'of Mathon,' one of Pershore Abbey's other major holdings. The Marmyun family also figure prominently on the Broadway roll, John, Nicholas and Robert rendering 19/10d in total. The Marmiuns' evidently once ranked among the premier families, although their connection with the village is all but forgotten. A Robert Marmiun of Bradeweye, presumably an ancestor, merits a mention in the *Curia Regis* Rolls of 1210 in connection with the raising of a levy in the county. He has the distinction to be the first Broadway resident we know by name, and probably ranked among its leading citizens at the time construction began on St. Eadburgha's church. He is thought to be the same Robert Marmiun who as 'Justice Itinerant' collected fines on behalf of the county for the royal court, and was Sheriff of Worcester in 1186. This marks him as a man of wealth and position in the kingdom. The *Dictionary of National Biography* states that his family reputedly held the hereditary office of King's Champion, whilst Robert himself served Richard the Lionheart in that capacity. He was with the King at Normandy in 1195, and two years later witnessed the treaty between King Richard and Baldwin of Flanders. Robert took a vow for the Crusades, but later purchased exemption, and after Richard's death in 1199 sided with the barons against Richard's brother, King John, during the turbulent years which led to the drafting of the Magna Carta. On John's death in 1216 he rejoined the royal fold, and died peacefully two years later. A 16th century lease describes land, believed to be that on which the 18th century Tower now stands, as *'Willet me Marmun heath;'* seemingly a reference to this once important Broadway family.

(Opposite: Appointments to the Manor Court 1757)

We Apoint for the year insueing } Mich:ll Russell Constable

We Apoint) W:m Staite
) Jn:o Bloxham   Tythen Men
) Rob:rt Carless

We Apoint) Rich:d Ricketts
            Simon Ansell   Ale Tasters

We Apoint) Frances Greenhill
            Rich:d Scrogg   Brick Baylies

We Apoint) W:m Phillipps
            W:m Agg   Field Stewards
            Jn:o Bloxham

We Apoint) Rob:rt Carless
            W:m Bloxham   Compt takers
            W:m White

We Amearce) Ed. Cotterell for his   £ s d
             Piggs going out (Conterary to Order)   0 1 7

We Amearce) Frances Tandy for Dameging
             the Common Stream Conterary   0 11 10
             to Order by Shuting in the Brook

We Amearce) M:r Cotterell Brook for putting
             Cows in to the Pasture un-nabed   0 11 10
             Conterary to Order

In the 14th century hereditary surnames were still the exception, and mainly the preserve of the wealthy. Their emergence among the general population was a gradual process which spanned several centuries. Surnames of the ordinary citizens were predominantly informal nicknames employed to better identify the various Johns, Roberts and Alices of the parish. Typically they referred to a person's trade, place of origin or abode, or some personal characteristic, not always a flattering one. This is often helpful when analysing medieval documents. If we employ this assumption, we can surmise that in 1280 Broadway counted among its inhabitants, two millers, *(Hugh and Simon Molendinario)*, a pigman, *(John Hogeman)*, two horsemen, *(John and Jordan le Horsmon)*, and several smiths or *Fabros*. The distaff side included several widows *(relicta)*, Christina the widow of Roger the Shepherd *(Bercarii)*, and Christina the Quarrier, who presumably worked one or more of the stone quarries dotted about the Broadway hills. One such, noted in a 14th century document, carried the obscure name of *Gunberspitt* (Gunber's Pit). A *quarre breche*, located it is thought close to Middle Hill, is mentioned in later records.

The last name on the tax roll is William le Somenur, whose surname indicates him to be a member of a particularly detested class of cleric. A summoner's job was to issue punishments for sins not recognized by the lay court, for example evasion of tithes, the disregard of sacraments, and sexual incontinence. Trevelyan notes that penances issued by summoners were routinely commuted for payment in cash, from which official practice it became just a short step to blackmailing sinners in their own homes. Their disreputable reputation was well-established by the 14th century, as Chaucer had one character remark in his Canterbury Tales:

'Art thou than a bailiff?' 'Yea,' quod he
He dorste not for veray filth and shame
Say that he was a Sompnour, for the name.'
(Friar's Tale)

Chaucer's unflattering portrait has the summoner come to town to threaten a poor old widow with a false summons, by which device he hopes to extort a fine. There he falls in with a fiend, the devil's agent, and they agree to share the proceeds of their evil deceptions. The widow, unable to pay, curses the summoner saying that the devil might take him. Justice triumphs as the fiend, taking the widow at her word, carries off the summoner to his just reward.

Turnpike House in the Upper High Street. The road between Evesham and the summit of Fish Hill became a toll-road as a result of legislation dated 1728. (Photo: B. Parsons)

Later Subsidy Rolls indicate that Broadway was not a static society, but a dynamic one where the fortunes of individuals and families rose and fell. Given the uncertainty of day-to-day existence this is hardly a surprise. For Broadway as a whole, the early 1300's marked a high point. Thereafter its fortunes mirrored the general decline in population and trade that characterised the 14th and 15th centuries. Between 1308 and 1322 a catastrophic series of wet summers caused distress throughout Britain. Crops rotted in the fields, cattle and sheep fell prey to disease, and between 1315-1317 the country was seized by a terrible famine. People were reduced to living on carrion and many starved for want of sustenance. Others were murdered by bands of hungry robbers who roamed the countryside searching for food. The great suffering is obliquely indicated by the grant of a licence about the year 1320 from the Bishop of Worcester to the monks of Pershore reconciling their cemetery from the effusion of blood and homicide. Clearly there had been some horrific event nearby that required the issue of this licence. It is not hard to imagine that, as traditional providers of alms to the needy, the monks would have borne the brunt of actions by desperate mobs. In 1327 the monks further petitioned the Bishop that the scarcity of the previous few years, combined with disease and murrain among the sheep, had so reduced the capacity of their house they were unable to put the church and conventual buildings into repair.

Misery was then piled upon distress. In June 1348 the Black Death, or 'Great Pestilence,' arrived in England. Transmitted by fleas and transported by the (then) ubiquitous black rat it spread rapidly from its port of origin on the southern coast, to reach parts of the Midlands by November 1348. Contemporary accounts of the disease report that it killed without discrimination, young and old, rich and poor alike. Whilst estimates of the final death toll vary, most historians now accept that between one third and one half of the entire nation perished, perhaps two million in all. Few records have survived, but the Register of Wolstan de Bransford, Bishop of Worcester from 1339-1349, provides a hint of the full horror locally. In his Memorandum of Appointments to Midland parishes falling vacant by reason of resignation or death, thirteen vacancies were notified between the months of January and July 1348. For the identical period during 1349 the figure was a startling two hundred and four. The greatest number of entries fall during May, June and July 1349, when one hundred and fifty one parishes of the diocese fell vacant.

The progess of the disease can be examined by studying the list of affected parishes. The rector at Little Rissington was replaced on 1 June 1349, and new appointments followed in swift succession at Atherstone, Alcester, Stratford-on-Avon, Alderminster, Exhall, Bidford, Little Compton, Upper and Lower Slaughter as well as dozens more villages and towns in the surrounding area. On 1 July the rector of Broadway, Henry de Burgh, was reported to have died and was succeeded by William de Okleye, his 'poor clerk'. De Okleye was probably then living under the patronage of Henry de Bradeweye a prominent citizen with estates at Oakley in Hampshire. The sudden death of the rector allowed him an unexpected opportunity for preferment, though it was all too temporary. Soon he too was dead, replaced on 13 October by John de Askham at the instigation of King Edward III, the temporalities of Pershore Abbey being by then in the King's hands. Clearly, the Abbey had not escaped the plague's evil effects. During that same July week vacancies were also notified at Mickleton, Buckland, Wormington, Stanton, Childswickham, Pebworth and Willersey, indicating that the immediate district was being ravaged. It is not possible to say how many died at Broadway, but there is no reason to suppose its citizens enjoyed any special immunity. On 6 August 1349 the Bishop's register fell abruptly silent as he too succumbed.

Broadway High Street and adjacent fields at Enclosure, 1771.

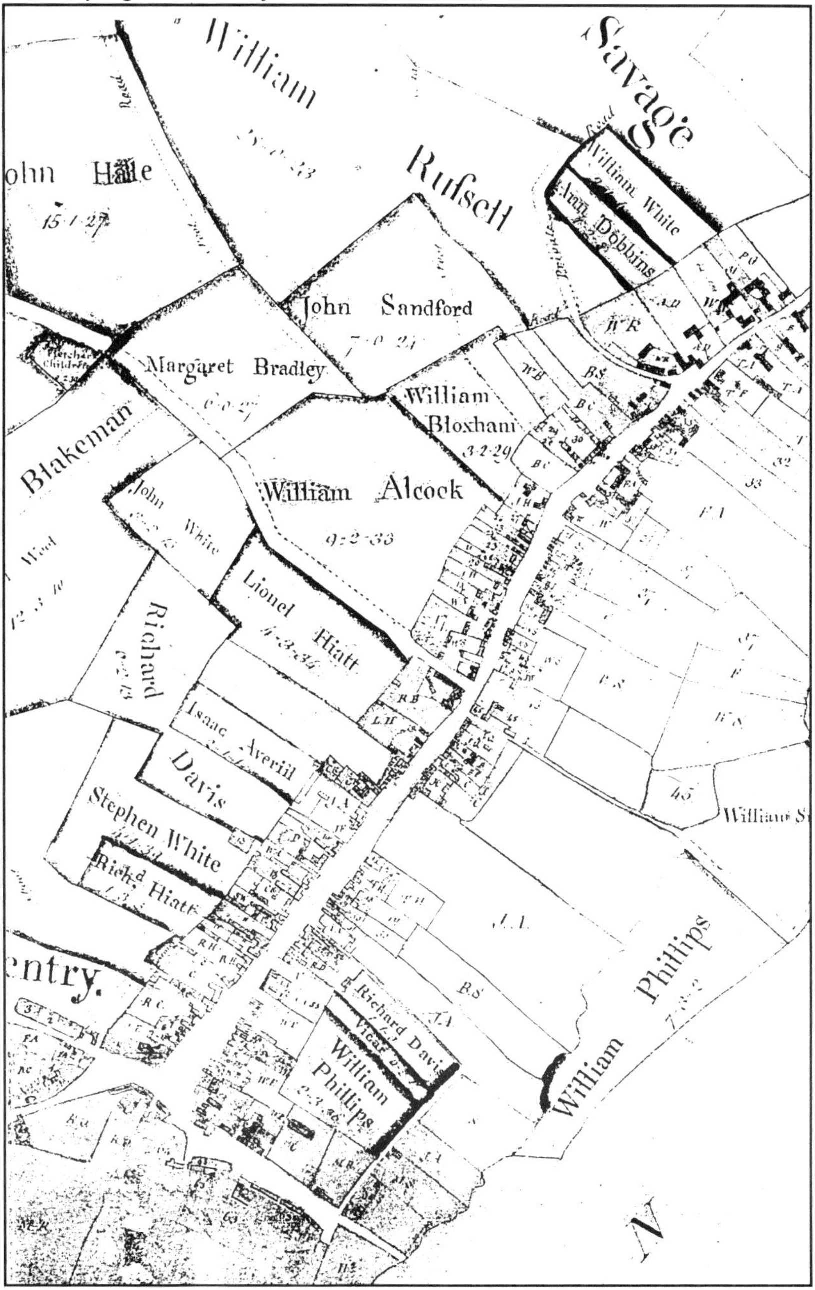

The 'Township' of Broadway

Mr. Bridgeman, Schoolmaster, supervises boys at the Leamington Road School. Pike Row cottages which stood by the Leamington Road Turnpike, can be seen in the background.

The sudden collapse in population did not, as expected, bring chaos. Instead, it relieved the intense pressure that had built up on land resources during the previous two centuries. For the lucky survivors the standard of living actually rose, as it was no longer necessary to cultivate marginal land, and the better acres were shared among fewer people. For a time there was a move away from a cash economy and a return to prosperous self-sufficiency. The decline of serfdom was also hastened as previously oppressed peasants deserted their holdings, taking advantage of more attractive opportunities on other manors, or quickly becoming prosperous enough to purchase their freedom. Broadway, although probably a smaller community, became one where the average citizen enjoyed a much improved standard of living.

For the landlord class, however, heavily dependent on rents and customary service, the Black Death proved a severe misfortune. With fewer and increasingly truculent tenants, often with the benefit of long fixed-rate leases at advantageous rates, and a rebellious villein class, the control of estates became progressively more difficult. The decline in demand for land on the Worcestershire, Gloucestershire and Warwickshire estates of the bishopric of Worcester was so severe that by the 1430s tenants were able to withhold payment of rent on a grand scale, and disputes became commonplace. In 1458 John and Elizabeth Stanley challenged Edmund Hert, Abbot of Pershore, over the control of a thousand acres of sheep pasture lying between Broadway and Chipping Camden. The Abbot

Lyebrook cottages, by St. Eadburghas, destroyed by fire in the 1970's. (Photo:J Parsons)

protested to the King that his tenants had unjustly 'cut him off from his holdings and his villa [presumably Abbots Grange] in Bradway'. The Abbot did however manage to regain possession of his property, and the Stanleys' were ordered to pay him forty shillings and 'go quietly away.'

Pershore Abbey was dissolved on 24 January 1539, and for the next century or so, village life was dominated by the Sheldon and Savage families. In 1575 Ralph Sheldon of Beoley purchased, from Sir William Babington, the Broadway lands granted by lease to his grandfather, Ralph Sheldon of Abberton, in 1538. Sheldon borrowed heavily to finance the purchase, and was thus obliged in 1577 to dispose of large parts of the Broadway estate to meet his debts. This he did, by lease or sale, to more than a dozen local farmers. He thereby multiplied the number of yeoman freeholders many-fold and is thus credited with furthering the growth and ultimate beautification of the village, which resulted from the new owners constructing substantial houses appropriate to their newly-assumed status. Despite both wealth and position, neither the Sheldons nor the Savages were well regarded locally. The Sheldons were far too disputatious in their dealings with others, and of their near cousins it was obscurely said; *'there never was but one good Savage, and he was hanged on Dunnington Heath !'*

From the time of Elizabeth I, the population of Broadway grew quickly, reversing the late-medieval decline. Parish registers indicate that it more than doubled between 1550 and 1620 by which time it exceeded seven hundred. After this remarkable turnabout there followed a curious and, as yet, unexplained fall in population which lasted for something like half a century. This ran counter to the national trend. It is suggested there was a switch at this time from labour-intensive subsistence farming to land-intensive sheep farming, perhaps as the result of commons enclosure following Sir Thomas Coventry's purchase of large parts of the Savage estates around 1620. Whatever the cause, the village itself continued to prosper, as witnessed by the fact that during this period some of its finest houses were built. By 1660, John Ogilby, the famed mapmaker, was able to describe Broadway as: *'A well-built town of 5 furlongs length affording several good Inns for accomodation.'* The largest of these inns, indeed the largest of the village buildings, other than the Manor House, were the White Hart (now the Lygon Arms) and the newly-built Angel Inn (Tudor House) which contained respectively twelve and thirteen hearths according to contemporary Hearth Tax returns.

The Post-Restoration period ushered in the great coaching era, during which Broadway's economy was transformed as it capitalized on its strategic location on the main Worcester to London road. Traffic on Britain's roads continued to grow as the Industrial Revolution took hold, and this proved greatly to Broadway's advantage. The particular requirement for wagons and coaches to couple additional horses in order to mount Fish Hill helped establish Broadway as a coaching centre, as well as a convenient place to halt for rest and refreshment. The focus of activity therefore began to shift from subsistence agriculture towards servicing the needs of passing trade; a trend that continued into the 18th century. One noticeable result was a dramatic increase in the number of public houses in the village, which at one point exceeded thirty. The number of artisans and tradesmen working in the village also increased, as is evident from the parish records. In 1686, following the death of its benefactor, Thomas Hodges, a charity school was established for the education of 'twenty poor boys,' the first indication of formal schooling in the village. Hodge's Charity still exists, and today provides bursaries to students. The old way of farming finally came to an end in 1771, when the remaining common land of the Upper End was enclosed by Act of Parliament.

For most rural communities, Enclosure foreshadowed the impoverishment of their labouring poor, and led to depopulation. Broadway's experience was entirely different. Enclosure in fact proved the catalyst for further expansion of its commercial base, and between 1770 and 1840 the number of inhabitants doubled to almost seventeen hundred, reaching five times the number it had been just three centuries earlier. Broadway in effect burgeoned into a substantial village, a town perhaps, and even adopted, it is thought during the early 1800's, the pretension of a Town Crier.

CHAPTER FOUR

CHURCH AND RELIGION

Of Broadway's few surviving medieval church buildings, St. Eadburgha's, a plain Norman church of red sandstone ashlar and rubble, is considered the oldest. Its central tower dates from around 1180; the north and south transepts being late 13th century additions, and the upper part of the tower, which houses the bells, dating from about 1400. The plain circular bowl-shaped font is thought to be original, and the church is generally believed to have replaced an earlier Saxon house of worship.

St. Eadburgha, to whom it is dedicated, was the daughter of the Saxon King Edward the Elder and the grand-daughter of Alfred the Great. Whilst commonly represented as a nun, recent research has discovered that before taking the veil she was married (c. 937) to Alberic, Duke of Colombe, and had a son, Bouchard de Montmorency, thus giving her, despite her Saxon origins, acceptable Norman credentials. After her husband's death she became abbess of a nunnery near Winchester and led a very holy life, for which she was subsequently canonized. She was adopted as an icon by the monks of Pershore, and was buried at the Abbey. The church at Leigh, another of the Abbey's estates, is also dedicated to her.

Prior's Manse, is another of Broadway's rare medieval survivors. An early 14th century stone building, with Elizabethan additions, it stands at the junction of the High Street and Leamington Road. It is said to have housed the steward of the Abbot, and until about 1870 a large barn, probably a tithe barn, stood adjacent to it on land now occupied by the Police Station and Library.

Abbots Grange, which overlooks the village Green, dates from about 1320. Now largely obscured by a hedge, it is usually described as the

Church and Religion

Priors Manse, at the junction of High Street and Leamington Road, dates from about 1320, and is said to have housed the Abbot of Pershore's steward. A large tithe barn once stood adjacent, and is noted on the Enclosure map. (Photo: B. Parsons)

summer residence of the Abbot of Pershore. It suffered mixed fortunes after the Reformation. Whilst its use during the 17th century is unknown, during the 18th and early 19th centuries it was the Poor House, and housed some thirty poor folk of the village. Its cellar was, at the same time, used as the village lock-up, suspected felons being held there awaiting their appearance before the Justices at Worcester. An entry in the Overseers Accounts for 1820 which reads *'Straw for the hole, 6d,'* indicates the rudimentary nature of bedding provided for prisoners. During the 19th century, the house fell into virtual ruin and was later restored by the American artist, Frank Millet, who drowned in the Titanic disaster in 1912. Today it is a private residence.

Barnard records that during the early 13th century, Ranulf, Prior of Worcester, built a chapel in the village in honour of the Holy Trinity, and ordered the Dedication Feast to be held on Wednesday in Whitsun week. The chapel is believed to have occupied the site of St. Michael's and All Angels church in the Snowshill Road, and consequently stood at the entrance to the Upper End of the village. It was replaced in 1608 by a small, stone chapel described by Prattinton in the 19th century as having a bell-turret, wooden roof but no ceiling, and containing a pulpit of blue and gold.

Abbots Grange, circa 1890, in a truly dilapidated state. This photograph shows its church-like features. (Supply: Worcester County Record Office)

Church and Religion

The 15th century octagonal pulpit from the earlier chapel was removed to St. Eadburgha's. The later chapel was replaced in 1839 by the present church of St. Michael's, which is still known locally as the 'New Church' in order to distinguish it from the 'Old Church' of St. Eadburgha's.

Although Broadway has apparently always been well endowed with religious houses, the practice of religion in the village has a somewhat chequered history. The inability of Pershore Abbey to properly regulate its affairs over many centuries naturally had a detrimental effect on the support of religion in its manors. The scandals and misfortunes suffered by the Abbey were many. In 1223 it was completely destroyed by fire, not for the first time, and seriously damaged in 1288. The Great Famine of 1315-1317 severely affected the Abbey and its manors. In 1340 the Bishop of Worcester committed custody of the Abbey to the previous Abbot, on the grounds that certain 'degenerate sons' were wasting its goods and creating grievous scandal by applying them to their own licentious pleasures. In 1352 Pope Boniface IX stated that the monastery was weighed down with debt and in need of repair. Two centuries later, it seems matters had not improved. In 1526, the new abbot, John Stoneywell, discovered the Abbey had enormous debts, much of the responsibility for which he placed at the door of Christopher Westerdale, the elderly bailiff of Broadway, who Stoneywell accused of using his position to plunder the monastery of silver plate, pots, spoons and jewellery amounting to several hundred pounds. He further accused Westerdale's wife, Elizabeth, of an improper relationship, *'unlawful familiarity...as the common fame is,'* with the former abbot. He refused payment of certain bills, and stopped the pension of Robert Bishopp, the late vicar of Broadway, who sought redress in the royal court. Stoneywell did however succeed in rescuing the Abbey from debt, only to see his efforts frustrated when Henry VIII dissolved the Abbey and seized its property in 1539.

Broadway lies at the very southern tip of Worcestershire, and the manor fell under the Archdeaconry of Gloucester, itself part of the Diocese of Worcester. The Abbot of Pershore, although autonomous in his daily duties, was therefore answerable to the Dean of Camden, and ultimately to the Bishop of Worcester for the responsible management of his estates. During the medieval period, estates were policed by the Bishop who made frequent circuits of the Diocese, which allowed him to investigate irregularities and controversies brought to his attention. Bishop Wolstan de Bransford is recorded as having visited Broadway in February 1340 where he dined and rested the night. It is supposed he may have sojourned at the Manor House or Abbots Grange. He returned in November 1342 summoning local clergy, and others, to assemble for examination at Childwickham church. Required to attend were the heads of religious houses, portionists (ie. those appointed to church sinecures), deans, rectors, clerks, and holy water bearers from the churches, chapels and oratories (private chapels), of Childswickham, Stanton, Buckland, Broadway, Hinton-on-the-Green, and Aston Somerville. Requested to attend from every parish were four, and from every chapel, two or three, trustworthy parishioners likely to have knowledge of matters requiring correction and reformation. Either there were few causes for complaint, or the chosen representatives were too timid to air their grievances, since several centuries of records indicate just one complaint against an abbot touching on Broadway. In 1269, we find a mandate issued by Bishop Giffard to the Dean of Campden compelling Abbot Henry de Bideford of Pershore, his cellarer, and their bailiffs of Broadway, to make restitution to the executors of the will of Adam de Cestreton, late rector of Broadway, for goods they had carried off.

The Reformation and its immediate consequences was a further cause of disruption to everyday worship in Broadway. William Babington's purchase

Shear House, the former Vicarage in Leamington Road, pictured here in 1968. The house was demolished to make way for retirement accommodation.   (Photo: B. Parsons)

of the manor in 1558, which included the advowson (the right to appoint the rector and the income from the rectory,) clearly led to a neglect of the church. The early parish registers contain gaps which coincide pretty nearly with his period of ownership; and as further evidence, an unknown hand later offered the following explanation for the omissions:

'N.B. these vacancies were occasioned by the small and insufficient maintenance ye vicarage afforded. Great part of the parish being Abbey land which together with ye tythe were disposed of blindly without regard to ye credit and support of Religion by that lustful beast King Henry VIII.'

Babington was an absentee landlord, and as such might have been expected to neglect his responsibilities. Sadly, although the manor soon fell into the ownership of local families, matters did not greatly improve. A memorandum states that profits from the vicarage were lapsed to the Crown in 1646, during the Civil War, and not restored until 1693. In 1703 the income was a mere £17 per annum. Under the stewardship of Reverend John Griffiths, vicar from 1706 - 1736, the living was at last augmented, largely due to the benefaction of a Mr. John Foster, tobacconist, of New Palace Yard, Westminster. Foster's connection with the village is unknown. The appointment of the rector later became the responsibility of the Peache Trustees. A schedule dated 1715 described the church land and property, which then included *'one dwelling house with a garden and backside, and three leys lying at the backside...by the name of the Crofts...one moiety* [half] *of the tythe lambs issuing and falling on one hundred and twelve yards land in Broadway...three quarters of a yard land dispersed in the common fields of Broadway and known by the name of Sheldons.'* The three fields, known collectively as the Crofts, are now part of the car park off Church Road. The dwelling house, referred to in the schedule, stood adjacent to the Jacobean chapel. Although it no longer exists, the Enclosure map (1771) shows it to have been a substantial residence set some distance back from the road.

The Commonwealth years (1649-1660) witnessed an increase in non-conformists, of which the most visible and controversial group were the Society of Friends, - or Quakers as they were then derisively known. Founded in 1647 by George Fox, the son of a weaver from Drayton-in-the-Clay, the movement spread quickly despite the persecution suffered by its adherents. Quakers alienated the establishment by their refusal to pay tithes,

The village Co-op Shop stood adjacent to Priors Manse at the junction of High Street and Leamington Road. It was demolished in 1971, and the road widened. (Photo: B. Parsons)

swear oaths in a court of law, use Church of England ministers for services, or uncover their heads in the presence of their 'betters.' Their religion also embraced all classes without discrimination and gave an equal place to women.

Broadway had Quakers among its inhabitants, although they were not a large group. William Webb was a known member. It is said that in 1657, while passing through Chipping Campden on his way to a meeting, he was observed by a Justice of the Peace who demanded ten shillings from him for travelling on a Sunday, and for non-payment ordered him to be put in the stocks. In 1662, a lieutenant with a party of trained bands, (members of the county militia), came to a Broadway meeting and commanded those who were met there to disperse. One of them, Robert Bayliss, did not move quickly enough and the lieutenant drew his sword. This so terrified Bayliss's wife, who was nearing confinement, that she was put in great fear of her life.

Bayliss was evidently a man of some means; his house was assessed at four hearths in contemporary tax returns. John Freeman, another known member, was by contrast a poor man who we find in receipt of parish relief in 1693 when 'visited by the smallpox.' William Sambach the Elder, of the illustrious local family of that name, was another known member. These latter two friends died in 1710 within a few days of each other. The burial register for that year records that '*John Ffreeman an old Quaker dyed and was put in ye ground, Nov 27,*' - without benefit of service presumably; and on December 2nd, '*William Sambach, Quaker, died and was carried to Broad Campden.*' Broad Campden was a centre for Quakerism in the district, and a meeting house survives there to this day.

There is no record of an official Quaker meeting house in Broadway, but the dwelling house of Jacob Gibbs, husbandman, was licenced for services under the 1689 Toleration Act. The Act permitted freedom of worship to protestant dissenters, and thus ended forty years of persecution. A house and land on the south side of the upper High Street is described in 1771 as the property of the 'Society of Quakers,' but by 1824, when they seem to have died out as a group, the house is shown as under private ownership.

After the death of Reverend Griffiths in 1736, the Honorable Henry Savage succeeded. Savage, independently wealthy through his connection with the Middle Hill family, died in 1771 and his successor was the Reverend John Palmer M.A., incumbent of the Gloucester rectory of St. Michaels. Palmer served the parish for ten years, but left the day-to-day duties of the parish to a curate, as did his replacement Reverend Charles Crawley. Crawley inherited Palmer's appointee, the Reverend David Davies, curate from 1777 until his death forty two years later in 1819.

Davies was a controversial figure, known locally, for reasons it is unnecessary to elucidate, as 'the drunken parson.' He was not, it seems, a man remembered with great affection. John Morris, a village historian, who had the benefit of speaking to Davies' near contemporaries, records that the curate's behaviour towards his flock was not always that expected from a man of the cloth. This is confirmed by the existence of some rambling verses written by his long-suffering wife Lucy admitting to her husband's imperfections. The following story is told of him. It was the custom to charge for reading prayers for the visitation of the sick. These were regarded as a passport to a better land. On one occasion, having been summoned to perform this duty for a dying parishioner, Davies enquired of the family, '*Have you got the shilling ?,*' and receiving a negative response replied, '*Let the old devil go to hell, then !*'

Reverend Davies' curacy coincided with a new wave of non-conformism. As the village grew after 1770, Roman Catholic, Congregational and Weslyan houses of worship were established. All still flourish today. The Congregational chapel, located on the south side of the High Street above

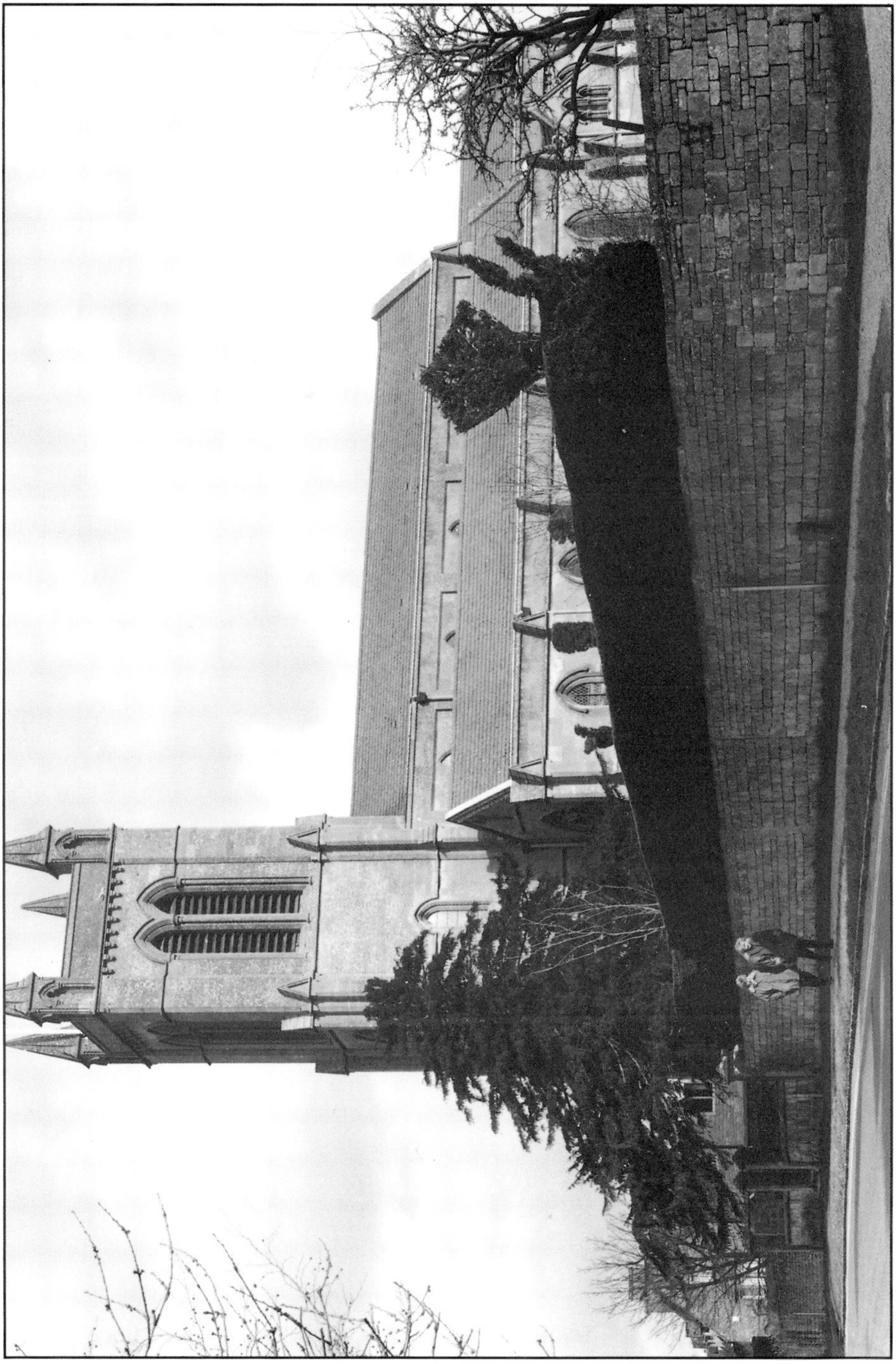

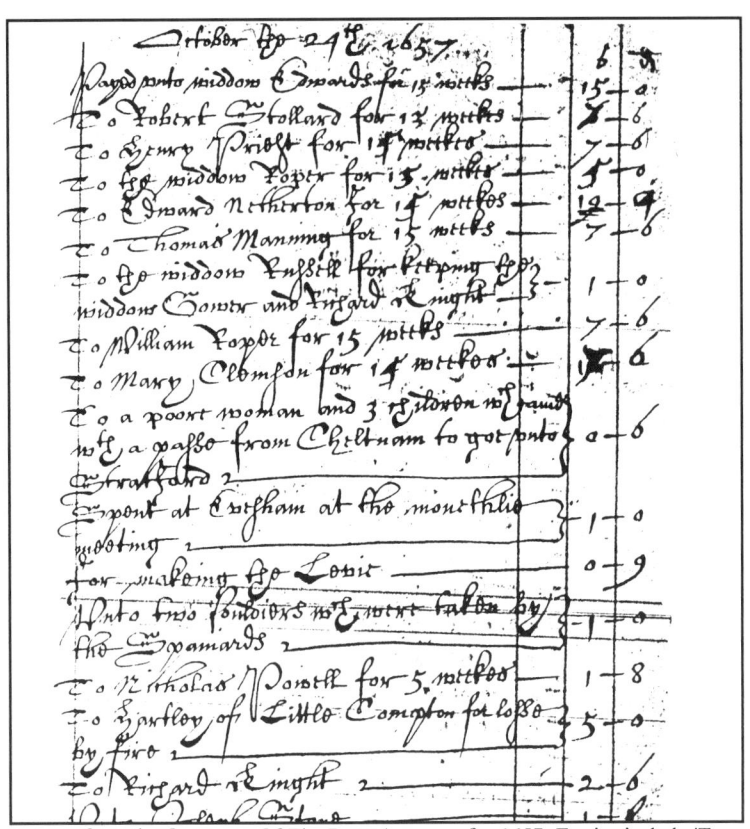

Extract from the Overseers Of The Poor Accounts for 1657. Entries include 'To a poore woman and 3 children who came with a passe from Cheltenham to go unto Stratford, 6d,' and 'Unto two of Welsbourne who had great losse by fyer, 1/-.'

the Willersey road turn, was built in 1798, and rebuilt in 1811. The Weslyan chapel, below Priors Manse, was also built in 1811. The Catholic church in Leamington Road was built around 1828 at the instruction of its pastor, Reverend John Birdsall of Cheltenham, through the bequest of George Taylor, who left £1500 to found a new mission. In 1850 it was purchased by the Passionist Fathers and converted into the present monastery. A new wing was added in 1910, and this has recently become private flats.

Davies was followed by a number of undistinguished curates. William Bedford served from 1819-1822, D. Perkins from 1822-1836, B. Hemming

Previous Page: St. Michaels and All Angels Church in the Snowshill Road. (Photo: B. Parsons)

from 1836-1838, Henry Grey from 1838-1840, Reverend J. B. Skipper from 1840-1841, and W. Battersby from 1841. In 1846, Samuel Franklyn was appointed curate, and in 1849 became the first resident vicar in almost eighty years. Franklyn retired in 1858 and was succeeded by the Reverend William English.

English was probably the most controversial clergyman to have served the parish. A gentleman of firm theological opinions and excitable temperament he quickly found himself at loggerheads with his flock. Relations foundered on his insistence that all parishioners should pay the customary Easter Pence, due to him as Vicar of Broadway, a matter he was foolish enough to pursue at law. In the space of four years he became embroiled in many heated exchanges with villagers. He twice found himself before the Evesham Magistrates charged with assault - both cases were dismissed - had the vicarage windows smashed by an angry mob; was hung in effigy from a gallows; had an attempt made on his life by an unknown gunman, who peppered the helmet of the policeman employed to guard him; was ridiculed by villagers in the street who shouted the nickname 'Holy Billy' after him; and was finally 'drummed' out of the village by the women and children of the parish who pursued the carriage banging their pots and pans, on his final departure.

His replacement, Charles Caffin M.A., was a man of very different character. He quickly restored the natural harmony that should exist between a reverend and his flock, and spent twenty five years happily in the service of the parish. He may be said to have re-established the Church of England's reputation in the village. To avoid a repetition of past difficulties, it became practice to present offertories from the Easter services to the vicar in lieu of Easter Pence. Caffin made a number of improvements to the church. During his tenure a full choral service and a surpliced choir was introduced, the Church School adjoining Tudor House was extended, and a new organ installed in St. Michael's. When he died in 1887, such was the regard for him locally that the shops closed for his funeral, whilst private houses drew their shutters as a mark of respect. A funeral bier donated by his widow, and dedicated to his memory, is kept in St. Eadburgha's. Caffin's successor, the Reverend F.A. Morgan, served the parish diligently for more than twenty years. Ill health forced his retirement in 1910. Morgan had cause to remember his inauspicious first visit to Broadway when considering whether or not to take the vacancy. The day, he later recalled, was dull and rainy, and his wife remarked, *'I should think you would never come to this wretched place !'* But the following day, the cloud lifted, the

Church and Religion

sun shone and the village looked beautiful. They quickly made up their minds to come, and never regretted it. Morgan was responsible for introducing the Parish Magazine, and it was during his encumbancy that heating was installed in St. Michael's church.

Opposite: St. Eadburghas Church
(Photo: B. Parsons)

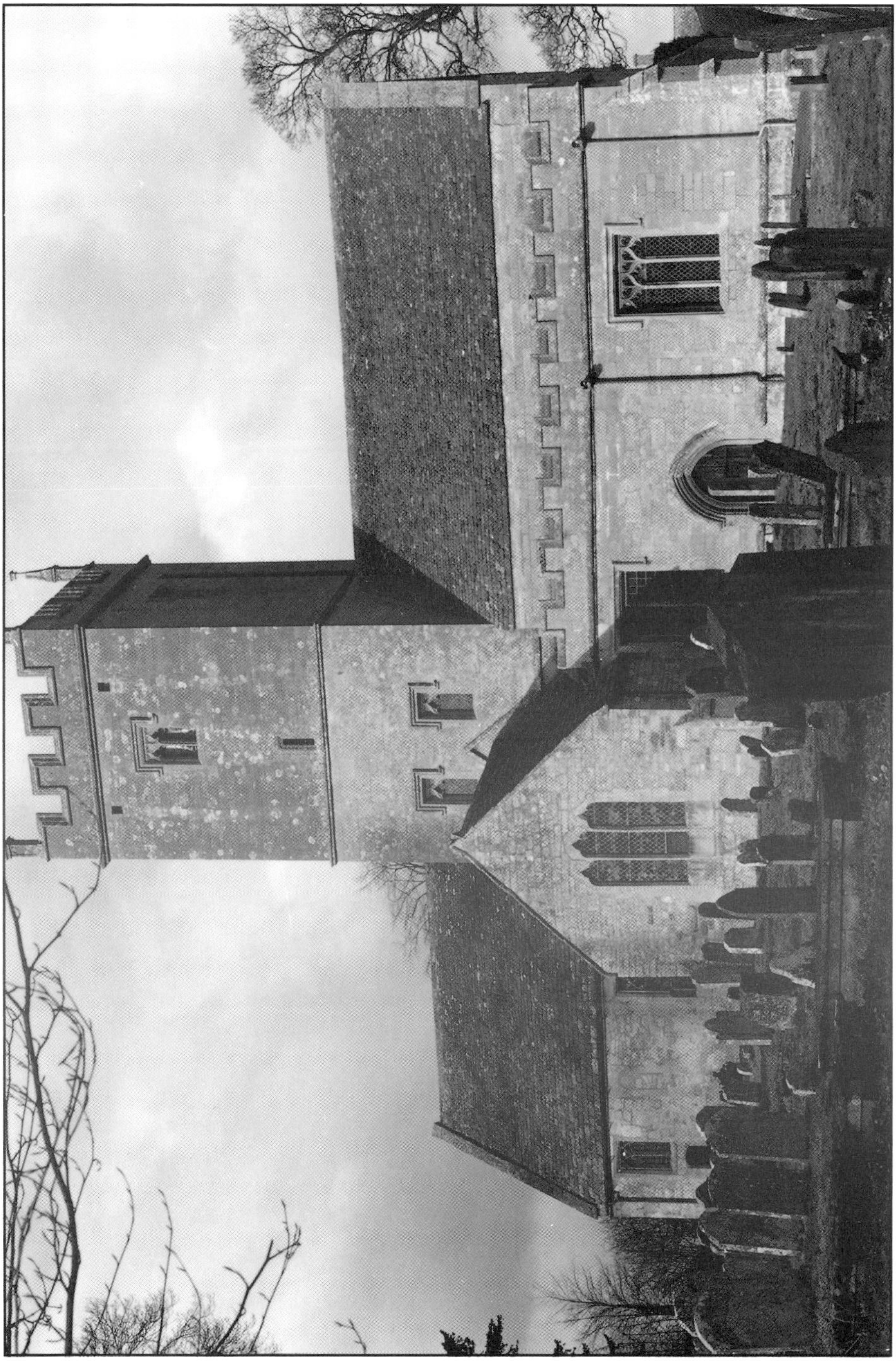

CHAPTER FIVE

MARKETS, FAIRS AND RECREATIONS

Broadway's modern Whitsun fair bears little resemblance to those of previous generations, though it nevertheless forms part of a long, and possibly unbroken, tradition of local markets and fairs dating from at least the 12th Century. A Pipe Roll of King Richard I records that in 1196, and during the two following years, the monks of Pershore were granted a weekly market on Wednesdays at Broadway, for which they paid ten marks. That the village was then sufficiently grand to warrant its own market is significant, if tempered by the suspicion that the grant formed part of a wider revenue-raising exercise, designed to enable the Exchequer to recoup monies extorted by the Emperor of Germany for the ransom of Richard I, and to fund Richard's madcap escapades in the Holy Land. In 1251, by which time Broadway is assumed to have received borough status, the Abbot was granted permission for a permanent weekly market at Broadway on Tuesdays, and a three-day Whitsun fair. Although the market has long-since failed, the latter survives as a fairground entertainment. The Abbot was, at the same time, granted 'free warren' over his lands, which conferred valuable rights to keep and hunt game.

Barnard records that in medieval times the Whitsun Dedication Feast was held in the following manner. The day would begin with a service of dedication at 4.00 a.m. followed by a morning devoted to prayer and good works, after which the feast was kept by every householder, *'each entertaining as far as in him lay such foreign acquaintances as would not fail when the like turn cometh about to requite him with kindness.'* Then came the sports and pastimes for which the English were renowned; football, skittles, bull-baiting, cambuc (a form of hockey), foot-races and wrestling. These rough entertainments were generally frowned upon by the church who made periodic, but largely unsuccessful, efforts to restrict

Markets, Fairs and Recreations

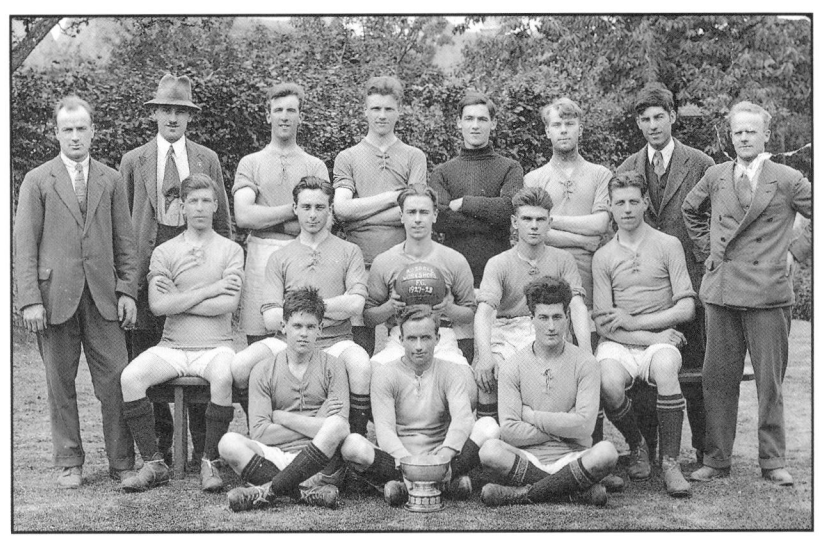

The Gordon Russell Workshop football team 1927/8

them. Whilst there are no records for Broadway, by-laws for the borough of Pershore dating from the end of the 14th century forbade its inhabitants from indulging in the 'unlawful' games of tennis, football and *'the dyse'* under pain of a 12d (5p) fine. Football was described as, *'nothing but beastly fury and extreme violence.'*

The weekly market at Broadway, which Nash noted in 1781 *'has long been disused,'* probably comprised the usual mixture of trade in animals, local produce and small items of manufacture. Sheep and wool were essential to the medieval economy of the Cotswolds, but there is no evidence of any significant market at Broadway. It is likely that sheep raised locally, - and these would have included separate flocks for the villagers, the Abbey, and the major leasehold tenants, - were sold at the larger Cotswold markets or, in the case of fleeces, perhaps traded directly with the London-based Merchant Staplers. There is no-one in Broadway's history to match the stature of William Grevel, the Chipping Campden wool merchant and financier to the King, whose fine Cotswold stone house graces its High Street. A contemporary of Grevel, and one of Broadway's leading citizens, was George de la Grove, alias George atte Grove, who we find mentioned in the 1332 Subsidy Roll, and again in the *Nonarum Inquisitiones* of 1340. In 1336 he acknowledged a debt of £120 to John de Stoke, parson of Saintbury church. The size of this sum suggests George was a merchant, the likelihood being he too traded in wool. Another

Broadway cricketers circa 1905 in assorted headgear. Dr. Haines, the vet, centre rear. Dr. Strandring in straw hat.

contemporary of Grevel was Henry de Bradeweye, who resided at Little Sambourne in Hampshire, and kept a substantial house in Broadway which contained a private chapel. De Bradeweye was probably both a major tenant of the Abbey, and a wool trader. It is recorded that Henry, and his wife, Agnes, died within days of each other in 1361, probably victims of a great plague which swept the country that year.

The 14th century marked the high point of the wool trade in England. Thereafter it declined, a victim of the slump in population which followed the Black Death. The rich grazing land of the Broadway Hills, however, remained a gathering place for sheep. In 1416, it is recorded that Abbot William de Newenton kept some fourteen hundred sheep there, including six hundred brought from his estates at Pershore and Leigh. The wool trade was a risky but potentially lucrative business. There are several references to local men being involved in the trade during the 15th century. One such was Thomas White, whose name is mentioned in the Stonor correspondence in 1478 when Thomas Betson, Merchant Stapler, pleads for payment for his goods from Dame Elizabeth Stonor, to settle a debt of four

Fundraising during the mid twenties at Madame de Navarro's to raise money for an ill-fated village swimming pool.

pounds for 'fells' (sheepskins) owed to 'Wyte of Bradway.' He is mentioned again in Chancery proceedings concerning an action for debt issued by 'Thomas Wyte of Broadway, husbandman,' against Thomas Wynnan, a London wool merchant, for twelve sacks of Cotswold wool Wynnan had ordered and kept for six years. This evidently formed part of a protracted dispute between the two men from which White emerged very much the poorer. By failing to respond to a royal summons which related to a counter-action for debt issued by Wynnan, White was outlawed by a decree of King Richard III. This effectively meant he could be killed on sight. On 10 June 1486, as an entry from the Calendar of Patent Rolls indicates, he was released from the charge after surrendering to the authorities:

'Pardon to Thomas White, late of Bradwey, under the Hill, husbondman, alias of Bradwey atte Bury End by le Withe, 'yeoman,' alias late of Bradwey, Co. Worcester, of his outlawry in the husting of London for his non-appearance before Richard III to satisfy Thomas Wynnan, citizen and wolman of London, of £20 and his fellows, late justices of the Bench of Edward IV; he having now surrendered to the Marshalsea prison, as William Huse, knight, chief justice, has certified.'

The danger for unsophisticated provincials when they tangled with the powerful Merchant Staplers is well illustrated. White's fate would have been to languish in prison until his debt was cleared.

Another local family connected with the wool trade, although rather more successfully, were the Sambachs; prominent gentry who leased, at one time, the Manor of Snowshill. In 1474, William Sambach of Bradewey gifted his worldly goods and chattels within the realm to Richard Wode, the Prior of Studley in Warwickshire. In connection with the gift reference is made to Philip Hardbene 'merchant of the staple of Calais', and Robert Hondy, a known Broadway wool producer and trader. Hondy (or Handy) became, jointly, the major leaseholder of abbey land in Broadway following White's decline.

The weekly market probably failed during the 15th century, as the population and trade dropped away. The annual fair, in part a market, survived but was for many centuries a modest affair. Nash described it as *'only for trifling articles.'* With the growth of the village during the early 19th century it again grew in importance, particularly the games and sports associated with it. John Morris recalled one of the crueller entertainments of earlier times before a more enlightened attitude gained sway.

'Bull baiting took place on the village green till about 1830. I have talked with old men who remembered not only a large stone with a ring in it that was fixed to the middle of the green to chain the bulls to, but who also remembered the baiting of the bulls with dogs. Privileged spectators then sat on the leads of the shop windows opposite, from which position they could watch the sport over the heads of the crowd, and see the unfortunate dogs go up in the air. On one occasion the bull broke its chain, and the spectators quickly dispersed and the bull revenged itself by upsetting the erections of the wake.'

In the gentler entertainments of the late Victorian period, the highlight was acknowledged to be the wheelbarrow race. The stream which runs the length of the High Street, and is now covered, was still open prior to about 1875, and the greatest fun was said to be watching the men in their barrows run into the brook.

The Whit Week celebrations continued locally with Dovers Hill Games. These were originated around 1610 by Robert Dover, a Warwickshire attorney, as an antidote to the prevailing puritanism. Held on the Thursday

A faded image from a forgotten age. Villagers gather on Broadclose Field to celebrate Queen Victoria's Jubilee.

and Friday of Whit week in fields above Chipping Campden, and thus following on from events at Broadway, they consisted principally of horse and pony races, on which one could bet, and such unusual not to say hazardous physical challenges as pate-cracking and shin-kicking, on which one could also bet. The latter event is said to have crippled many a local man. A report on the 1771 games remarked that festivities were conducted with the usual decorum, the 'rustics' displaying amazing courage and resolution in their respective talents of cudgelling and wrestling. The games were held, with breaks, for almost two hundred and fifty years until, by 1851, they had become so riotous an excuse was found to end them. They have since been revived and are again conducted in an orderly fashion. Shin-kicking is apparently still practiced, although pate-cracking no longer features.

The Whitsun games were just one of many opportunities for recreation in the village. Football and bowls have long been played. Golf has a more recent history, the club being established in 1895. Another popular pastime, at one time the preserve of the middle classes, was cricket. The game has medieval origins and was once banned for being detrimental to the practice of archery. Although the origin of the game in Broadway is unclear, the Victorian members of 'The Broadway and Evesham Cricket Club,' played regular fixtures by the 1850's. The modern cricket ground, opposite St. Eadburgha's church, only came into use this century. It is not apparent where games were previously held. Matches were, of course, taken very seriously, and the gentlemanly spirit with which cricket is still identified seemingly held sway. In August 1860 a return match at Broadway against Chipping Camden had a slow start when the 'Campdonians' refused to play. Their reluctance, it seems, was due to the presence of a certain gentleman player who had recently joined the Broadway club and was rated a 'don' in the art of cricket. It being thought unfair he should be fielded, the Campden men 'went to grass' and refused to budge. With no prospect of play, the teams instead set about their meal, provided by the landlord of the Bell Inn. A man was despatched to Campden to fetch one of the town's better players, and on his arrival, with the wine having induced a more congenial atmosphere, the match went ahead and was won by the visitors.

Hunting was popular in Broadway, particularly fox-hunting. The first known reference appeared in 1610 when William Sheldon remarked upon plans to join his father, William Sheldon the Elder, who was *'goeinge to huntinge the ffoxe with his hounds.'* During the 1860's the North Cotswold Hunt was created as a division of the Berkeley Hunt, and Broadway was chosen as its headquarters. The kennels are located at the end of the lane adjacent to Lloyds Bank. Hunting was immensely popular with all classes, and provided spectators and participants with a colourful and exciting spectacle. The social side included curiosities like the Earthstoppers' Dinner, and the Annual Hunt Ball, held usually at the Assembly Rooms of the Lygon Arms. At a meeting of the North Cotswold Hunt in 1881 the distinguished company included Lord Sudeley and Viscount Campden, the latter of whom lamented the increasing scarcity of foxes due to disease and the detrimental impact it was having on hunting.

Celebrations to mark coronations, royal marriages and jubilees, were greeted enthusiastically by a public largely starved of colour. These usually involved a procession through the streets, accompanied perhaps by a marching band, a dinner or tea for villagers in Broadclose Field in the centre of the village, followed by dancing and games. Later in the day, villagers would climb the hill to Broadway Tower, perhaps in a lantern procession, for a bonfire and fireworks. Immoderate drinking was often a feature of these occasions.

Markets, Fairs and Recreations

Broadway celebrated the Millenium of King Edgar's Charter in 1972. Shown here are two scenes from the Millenium day procession.
(Photos: J. Parsons)

The Victorian era was really the heyday of this type of celebration. There was a great scandal in 1838 when, on the Coronation of Queen Victoria, the wealthier inhabitants declined to include their poorer bretheren in the festivities. Their meanness of spirit, compared unfavourably to the generous treatment of the poor in neighbouring villages, was immortalised in a piece of anonymous doggerel. The penultimate verse declared, *'To ring the bells was their incline, To crack their jokes and drink their wine, While the Broadway poor did all repine, They had nothing at the Coronation.'*

This, fortunately, was an isolated example of parsimony. Subsequent celebrations invariably included the poorer villagers, indeed the day was usually centred around their enjoyment. The proceedings in 1871 to mark the marriage of Queen Victoria's daughter the Princess Louise, Duchess of Argyll, to the Marquis of Lorne, provide a good example. These included such genteel frolics as dipping for oranges and treacle rolls, sack racing, hurdling, wheelbarrow racing, sneezing for snuff, and racing for crinolines, followed by a balloon ascent. In 1893 on the marriage of Prince George of Denmark to Princess May, Reverend Morgan described the delightful scene.

'July 6th was a bright day in Broadway, and great thanks are due to Mr. Averill, not only for the field, where everybody enjoyed themselves, but also for the energy and heartiness which made the whole matter of our Feast so great a success. The many helpers always ready and kind, bringing out of the ample supplies one relay after another, as the Tent filled again and again, till children and aged folk and lastly those of any age tasted of the day's good things. The dancing, enjoyed all the more for the threat of rain at the beginning, was kept up merrily till 11 o' clock. During the last hour the hill was bright with Fireworks sent up by Mr. Flower from the Tower.'

The national rejoicing in 1887 to mark Queen Victoria's Golden Jubilee produced some of the most spectacular scenes of the century. In Broadway, following the usual festivities in the village, a lantern procession was made to the summit of Broadway Hill where an estimated four thousand people assembled to watch a bonfire and firework display. An observer at the top of Broadway Tower counted one hundred and twenty six other beacon bonfires.

The funds to pay for such celebrations were raised by public subscriptions, and it was the custom to use any surplus to provide for a lasting reminder of the occasion. In 1863, following celebrations on the

Markets, Fairs and Recreations

Crowds cheer King Edward VII as he passes Tudor House on a fleeting visit to Broadway in 1909. (Courtesy: T. Chinn)

marriage of the Prince of Wales (later Edward VII) to Princess Alexandra of Denmark, the local committee purchased brass instruments for the Church of England and Catholic school bands. A more permanent and visible monument was sought to mark the Golden Jubilee in 1887. Suggestions ranged from a lamp-post to a cottage hospital! After the usual protracted debate, and an examination of available funds, the committee agreed to the purchase of an illuminated bracket clock. This was erected on the National Schools building in the High Street where it can be seen today. It is affectionately known as 'the dummy' as its works are housed inside the building.

CHAPTER SIX

LAW, WAR AND DISTURBANCE

Broadway's peaceful tenor has been shattered but rarely during its long history. A few of the more memorable occasions are recorded below.

Broadway has, like any village, suffered the depredations of criminals down the ages, and although it has seldom harboured felons amongst its own number, there have naturally been exceptions. Its first identifiable rogue was a certain Walter Girre or Giror of Bradeweye, whose activities are chronicled in the Calendar of Patent Rolls of Edward III.

Walter lived during the early part of the 14th century, a period that had witnessed a decline in the traditional peasant culture. With it went that deep sense of mutual-dependence early medieval life had embodied. The feudal system was beginning to collapse generating stresses that were manifested by far greater instances of trespass, litigation and law-breaking.

The temporary chaos which followed the Black Death aided the dishonest, one such being Walter, who we find indicted, in 1354, before the Gloucestershire Justices of Oyer and Terminer, of plundering John, parson of Hynton [on-the-Green] church, of a horse, worth 10 marks, further plundering John atte Brugge, bailiff of the Abbot of Tewkesbury, at Kelveston, of 30 shillings of silver, and of being *'a notorious thief.'*

He was pardoned for these offences and *'subsequent outlawries'* on the word of the Duke of Lancaster, who stated that Walter was with him at Calais when the offences were committed. The reference here to the French port of Calais is interesting. These were the early days of the Hundred Years War with France. A memorable victory over the French had been won at Crecy in 1346, and Calais itself was besieged and taken in 1347. The

Milestone House in the upper High Street. The house to the right was the first Police Station. Previously, suspected felons were held in the cellar of Abbot's Grange. (Photo: J. Parsons)

likelihood is that Walter was a soldier, probably a mercenary, who despite an apparently ordinary background had somehow acquired the protection of the Duke, a cousin of the King. Whatever his guilt or innocence in the matter of the thefts, it would have been usual to pardon someone who had proved so useful to the Crown.

Apparently untroubled by his brush with justice, we discover Walter two years later, charged with involvement in a truly remarkable act of lawlessness. The Worcester commissioners reported, on the complaint of Thomas de Neubold, that *'William Spenser, 'chivaler', John Hondy of Upton on Severn, Walter Girre of Bradeweye, Robert, his brother,* (and more than a dozen others) *assaulted him at Worcester, trode down and consumed with cattle his crops and grass and felled his trees at Longedon* [near Upton-on-Severn], *carried away the trees with other of his goods, assaulted his men and servants there, and chased his tenants from the said town, and so threatened them that they dare not go to their own property to cultivate the lands and make his other profits there...'*

The case is astonishing because it demonstrates a complete disregard for the rule of law, - the suspects brazenly carrying off de Neubold's goods and terrorising those who offered resistance. All the more remarkable, the accused included a knight, a vicar and his chaplain. Spencer we know once held title to Longdon Manor, paying one knight's fee of 40/- for it in 1346. This suggests a dispute about ownership. Walter and his companions were probably thugs, hired to effect the return of his property. Unfortunately, judgement in the case has not survived, and nothing more is known of Walter or his brother Robert.

Direct action to remedy a perceived injustice was common in the days when a remedy at law was slow and expensive. But it sometimes had unfortunate consequences. In 1610 a dispute arose between the villagers of Childswickham and William Sheldon of Broadway over two fishponds Sheldon had dug a few years earlier on common land by Leedons near the Childswickham boundary. Sheldon was one of Broadway's two biggest landowners and, like many of his family, no respecter of persons. The story of the dispute can be found in depositions made to support a Star Chamber suit for damages issued on the part of villagers of Childswickham and Murcot.

The pools, which were fed by the Mill Brook, had for several years caused offence to the villagers. On a number of occasions water had flooded adjoining meadowland, damaging the hay they cropped for winter feed. The water had also been tainted. To attract game, which he would hunt with his hawk, Sheldon had caused carrion to be placed in the pools. The occasional overflow from this found its way back to the brook, polluting water that villagers used downstream for drinking, brewing and 'dressing' meat. A flood in 1607, caused it was thought by some sudden breach in the pools, had almost carried away two women washing clothes in the brook.

On 5 January 1610, their patience having finally expired, a party of villagers from Childswickham and Murcot assembled at dawn at the back end of Childswickham, armed with spades, shovels, mattocks and draining staves. Marching briskly to the pools they began to dig them down. Their task was almost complete when Sheldon, alerted by a shepherd boy, arrived on the scene with his servant Ambrose Cook. When he realised what was happening, Sheldon fell into a fury, as Thomas Combe later deposed, and struck William Combe, one of the diggers, a 'shrewd' blow with a shepherd's hook. He then demanded, *'Who sett you awork here ?',* adding, *'I discharge you and would see who dares digs here,'* whereupon John Gibbs of Murcot, aged 44, a husbandman, stepped defiantly down into a trench and said, *'That will I !'* Sheldon then struck him a great blow on the arm, and another on the head *'so that the blood did run about his ears.'*

Law, War and Disturbance

Sheldon despatched Cook to Broadway to summon reinforcements. Cook called first upon Baldwin Hodges who immediately came with him. He then paused at the house of William (later Sir William) Sambach who, diplomatically perhaps, declined to join them or furnish a weapon stating that he had none. Cook spied a staff in a blacksmith's shop on the village street, which he promptly requisitioned. The two men returned to find Sheldon still engaged in his argument. Cook later dramatically remarked that, had they not returned that instant, one of the diggers would have certainly slain Sheldon with an axe.

Within *'about halfe a quarter of an hower'* a dozen or more reinforcements arrived from Broadway armed with pikestaves and pitchforks. The trench-diggers then decided to abandon their work, and beat a hasty retreat along the Childswickham Road pursued by Sheldon and his men. In the violent melee that ensued the diggers were thoroughly routed. John Bowers, Sheldon's servant, struck Thomas Combe a heavy blow upon the shoulder with a pikestaff, *'soe that he was scarce able to stand upon his leggs,'* or as another described it, *'that he was redye to fall grovellinge on the grounde.'* Bowers also thrust Anthonie Whoodes, aged 40, severely in the buttock so that friends later had much ado to keep life in him. William Russell of Murcot, aged 35, was likewise stabbed by one of Sheldon's men, and returned home in a swoon. John Vickarridge ran at John Johnston with a large pikestaff hitting him in the thigh, and William Combe, still suffering from the blows meted out by Sheldon, received three or four more clouts about the neck with a stave. Laurence Hornebye, a disabled tailor from Murcot, whose only offence was to be passing at the time, was knocked down in the retreat. Sheldon's casualties were slight. Only Mr. Littleton Brace, a young gentleman of Hill Court, Dodderhill near Redditch, suffered any real injury. Struck by a stone, perhaps thrown by one of the Childswickham women who carried them in their aprons, he had fallen into one of the trenches. The Childswickham men being fleeter of foot than their pursuers, Sheldon and his party were eventually reduced to shouting abuse after them, to the effect that they were rogues, beggars, vagabonds and dastardly knaves, just that and nothing more. Thus ended the battle of the fishponds.

Previous page: A view of Broadway High Street. August 1899. The tranquil image belies the occasionally turbulent scenes the village has witnessed.
(Photo supplied: WCRO)

> *Aug.* 13, 1752.
>
> WHEREAS one THOMAS ROGERS, whom the Conftable of Broadway in the County of Worcefter was Yefterday conveying to the County Gaol, efcap'd from the faid Conftable; whoever will apprehend the faid Thomas Rogers, (fo that he may be fecur'd) fhall receive a Reward of *Five Pounds* from me,
>
> John Coleman, *Conftable.*
>
> *Note,* The above Thomas Rogers (who hath fometimes gone by the Name of *Thomas Moore*) is about 18 Years of Age, has fhort black Hair and black Eyes, of a very fwarthy Complexion, and about four Feet ten Inches high; and had on a white Linnen Frock, (a Flap of which is dawb'd with Pitch or Tar,) a blue Woollen Waiftcoat, with a newifh Pair of Buckfkin Breeches; and was charg'd with breaking the Mill-Houfe of Jofeph Smith, of Harvington.
>
> ⁂ He was very near the City of Worcefter when he efcaped from the Conftable, and is fuppofed to be gone towards *Napleton* or *Peopleton.*
>
> ―――
>
> *Stratford upon Avon, Warwickfhire.*
>
> THE Great FAIR for Cheefe, Seed-Corn, Hops, &c. which was annually held in this Town on the Thirteenth of *September*, and the two following Days

A Slippery Customer. Rogers was recaptured and transported.
(Courtesy: Berrows Worcester Journal)

Lying, as it did, between the two Royalist strongholds of Oxford and Worcester, Broadway saw much activity during the English Civil War. A year into the war, in September 1643, King Charles I, and his most loyal general, Prince Rupert of the Rhine, passed through Broadway heading for Stow-on-the-Wold. They rode in pursuit of the Earl of Essex, at the head of some 14,000 Cavalier troops. Essex was intercepted at Newbury in Berkshire where, on the 20 September, some 30,000 soldiers engaged in one of many inconclusive battles of the war. These vast transits of humanity often carried disease in their wake, and parish registers for Broadway indeed show an unusual increase in burials following the King's visit.

In June 1644 Charles passed twice over Broadway Hill. On the second occasion, Sunday 16 June, a Mr. Richard Symonds recorded in his diary that the King lay the night at the home of Mr. Savage in Broadway. This is assumed to be the long-since demolished Manor House in Bury End, at that time occupied by Walter Savage and his widowed mother. The background to his visit is interesting. In May 1644 Parliament resumed its offensive against the King, and despatched Essex and Sir William Waller to besiege Oxford. Charles, however, fled the city and headed for Evesham pursued by

Military Manoeuvres from a later era. Broadway Home Guard parade on the Village Green during the Second World War.

Waller and his men. By the time Waller reached Broadway, Charles was safely over the Avon at Evesham, and the pursuit was temporarily abandoned.

Charles then moved to Worcester, destroying the bridge over the Avon at Pershore in such haste that a royalist Major, two or three other officers, and twenty-six soldiers were drowned as it unexpectedly collapsed. Also drowned were several dozens civilian helpers whose hats were discovered floating down the river. The King reached Worcester on 6 June, where he rested for the best part of a week. Waller departed from Broadway and made his way, via a circuitous route, to Evesham where, to one senior royalist's disgust, *'the evil inhabitants received him willingly.'* He rested awaiting Charles's next move. On 12 June Charles left Worcester for Bewdley, giving the impression he intended to travel north and join with Prince Rupert. This was a ruse. He planned instead to return to Oxford, there to marshal his demoralised troops. Waller was deceived and left for Stourbridge. Charles returned to Oxford, via Broadway where he dined with Mr. Savage, pausing only long enough at Evesham to fine its inhabitants

£200 and a thousand pairs of shoes for their *'alacrity'* in receiving Waller. A few weeks later Charles finally engaged Waller in an inconclusive skirmish at Cropredy Bridge near Banbury. On 2 July, after removing to Moreton-in-Marsh, Richard Symonds relates that *'his majestie, with his whole army marched over the Cotswold hills, with colors flying &c., to Broadway; thence to Evesham that night, where he lay. On 12th July he returned whence he had come.'*

In 1645, Charles again went down by Broadway to Evesham en route to Droitwich, with Prince Rupert marching in the reargward. Hard on his heels came Colonel Massey who stormed the royalist garrison at Evesham on 25 May. The decisive battle at Naseby followed on 14 June. Prince Rupert and his troops were thoroughly routed and much of the royalist equipment captured. The siege and fall of Worcester in July 1646 marked a temporary end to hostilities in the Midlands.

The Midlands however was soon rife with discontent. Troops on both sides had not been paid for some time, and the political resolution of the war did not prove straightforward. In January 1647, junior officers of the Parliamentarian army met secretly at Broadway to discuss *'certain matters,'* in what became known as 'The Broadway Plot.' The principal evidence for a plot is contained in a letter, written in haste by an member of the Gloucester garrison, and read a few days later to the House of Commons. The communication concerned *'the complotting of some officers in a dangerous design about Gloucestershire, and the shires adjacent.'*

'A Council was held at Broadway the greatest part of last week by about eighty officers of Colonel Kempson's, Colonel Ayre's, Colonel Herbert's, and another regiment of foot; and of Colonel Cooke's regiment of horse. Their debate was upon their discontents, the surprisal of Gloucester, it being alleged that there were three hundred barrels of powder there, and they knew where to come at it, and that the works being bad they could easily surprise the town by night. Hartlebury Castle, they conceived, would be delivered to them by Colonel Turton. If not they held that easily surprised too. They had some discourse [as to] Ludlow, Shrewsbury, and Hereford, and an assurance that Langbourne would join them, and that they would have two thousand capmen from Bewdley, and also the discontented citizens of London would furnish them with present monies. To this debate there were about twenty dissenters, so that Saturday last they broke up their council, but it is thought that the rest who were for it will meet again, or have met sometime in the beginning of the week...'

Parliament was clearly alarmed by the communication. Fearing a renewed outbreak of hostilities in the Midlands they took immediate steps to halt the conspiracy. The garrison at Gloucester was relieved and Colonel Morgan's force there was removed to Stow-on-the-Wold.

King Charles was executed in 1649 and the royalist cause lost, if temporarily, when the future Charles II was defeated by Cromwell at the Battle of Worcester in 1651. Whilst no proof exists that Cromwell visited Broadway, he was at Evesham on, or about, the 27/28 August 1651, and again on 6 September after his victory at Worcester. He then returned to London by way of Chipping Norton, from where he wrote a letter on the 8 September. It is therefore likely that The Lord Protector of England, as he was later known, passed through the village on 7 September 1651, on his triumphal return to the capital.

****

The day-to-day responsibility for law and order in the village fell to the constable, a Manor Court appointee elected at the annual October meeting. The office itself dates from the 13th century. A constable's duties included the detection and apprehension of offenders, incarcerating them in the lock-up, carrying suspects before the local magistrate for examination, and if necessary transporting them, usually by wagon, to the county jail at Worcester to await judgement at the Assizes. Among his quainter duties was the raising of the 'hue and cry', which essentially involved alerting other parishes that a crime had been committed, and enquiring into the whereabouts of suspicious looking characters. This occasionally required the posting of notices of description and reward. The Broadway constable is recorded as having received one shilling in 1727 for *'going to Snowshill with a hue and cry.'*

The Constable's accounts for 1697/8 provide an insight into the nature and extent of his duties, which do not appear to have been especially arduous.

	£	s	d
The Accts of John Philips Constable of Broadway nominated and sworn at ye Court Leet holden there ye 15th October 1697 for ye year ensuing.			
Received upon four levies	17	8	0
Disbursed			
On ye acct of Sam Spurrier and Anne Birch when they were apprehended and carried to Goall for stealing Cows, - horse hire & all expenses	00	17	0
Ffor Apprehending again Samuell Spurrier & Will Spurrier for reseffing stoln goods, - for Carrying them before Sir Richard Cox at Dumbleton &c.	00	3	6
Ffor Taking Widow Spurrier & her son, Thomas Izod & Philip Ronsam before Sir Richard Cox. And Conveying Izod & Ronsam to Goall for horse stealing, all expenses	3	10	2
Ffor Taking John Barloe & Jeremy Smith & two women their Companions to ye Justice & conveying ye two men to Worcester on suspicion of robbing on Bourton hill at Stow fair in October	1	14	6
ffor Quarter Rates once paid in ye year	0	05	1
ffor all other Charges on ye Account of soldiers, Creples, hues & cryes, ye Charges of other officers & my self &c.	10	01	8
Total Disbursed	16	11	11
Remainder in hand	00	8	0

The 18th century brought a stiffening of attitudes towards crime in general and especially that against property. In 1780, for example, Sarah Roberts was sentenced to hang for stealing nine guineas, a half-crown, and some wearing apparel, from Robert Careless of Broadway. As was usual in these cases, she was reprieved and transported to the colonies. A public whipping awaited those convicted of lesser offences, such as petty theft and vagrancy; the Overseers Accounts Book for 1817 contains the purchase of a cat whip. As a deterrent to others, the sentence was usually carried out in the parish where the offence had been committed. The miscreant would either be tied to a whipping post, or to the back of a wagon which was then driven slowly through the streets. A post reputedly stood on the greens below the Swan Inn, although several cases refer to the latter method of punishment in Broadway. This painful form of entertainment was carried out by the constable, or by the county hangman, who was rewarded by onlookers with a literal 'whip-round.' Records indicate that Friday lunchtime was the favoured time for whippings at Broadway. In 1754 the Worcester justices ordered Richard White to be punished for stealing a sheet from Mrs. Harper. In 1784 Thomas Grove of Childswickham was whipped through the street for the theft of two ducks. Grove had been apprehended at The Spinning Wheel, a public house in China Square, with the ducks concealed in his capacious breeches. Unfortunately, the effects of this punishment were not always salutary. In Broadway churchyard lie the remains of a vagrant who offended the eye near Blenheim Palace. His burial entry, dated 19 June 1707, records that, *'Edward Child, a poor traveller punished at ye Woodstock as a vagrant, died in being carried to Childswickham.'*

In 1766 the village was rocked by the brutal murder of John Wynniatt, who farmed at Leedons near the boundary with Childswickham. His death may have been linked to the ending of the Seven Years War with France in 1763. This had brought widespread unrest to the country after renewed exports of grain caused bread and flour prices to rocket. Farmers and grain merchants were accused of exploiting shortages, and everywhere feeling against them ran high. The militia were deployed in several parts to quell riots, and even the 'poor' of Evesham, normally a peaceable bunch, were moved to concoct a plan to attack a local corn mill as a protest against high bread prices in local markets. Fortunately, their design was discovered, and suspected ringleaders were hauled before the Evesham magistrates to be threatened with transportation for life or execution, the draconian punishments for riotous assembly.

14

Scale of Rewards.

	£	s.	d.
For every incendiary, high-way robber, or house breaker, the sum of	20	0	0
For every horse-stealer, or cow-stealer, the sum of	10	0	0
For every sheep-stealer, pig-stealer, or person guilty of stealing goods, corn, or grain out of any house, barn, stable, or other building, the sum of	5	0	0
For every fowl-stealer, the sum of	3	0	0
For every person cutting down, lopping, or otherwise injuring timber or other trees, or young stands, persons breaking hedges, breaking and carrying away timber, gates, lifts, stiles, posts, bars, rails, stealing corn or grain, or any other goods out of the fields and yards the sum of	2	0	0

Scale of Subscription.

	Original Sub. £ s.	Annual Sub. £ s.
Professional gentlemen. Proprietors of land not exceeding 400 acres Occupiers of land not exceeding 100 acres. Tradesmen and all other persons who do not come under a higher rate of subscription	1 0	0 10
Proprietors not exceeding 800 acres Occupiers not exceeding 200 acres	1 10	0 15
Proprietors not exceeding 1200 acres Occupiers not exceeding 300 acres	2 0	1 0
Proprietors not exceeding 2400 acres Occupiers not exceeding 600 acres	3 0	1 10
Proprietors above 2400 acres Occupiers above 600 acres	4 0	2 0

Proprietors and occupiers of hill land, to be placed by the committee upon a lower scale, (*viz*) 3 acres for 1 acre.

Proprietors who occupy their own estates subscribe as occupiers; and proprietors who occupy part only of their estates, subscribe as occupiers for such part, and as proprietors for the remainder.

J. Grinnell, Printer, Broadway.

In the absence of an official police force, property owners made their own arrangements. This list of bounties dated 1838 is from a local Society for the Detection and Apprehension of Offenders.

Wynniatt's murder was a carefully planned act of violence, as a report in the *Berrows Worcester Journal* of 6 November 1766 makes plain.

'Last Tuesday fortnight, Mr. Wynniatt, of Leadings [Leedons], *in the parish of Broadway, in this county, was found in a field, near his own house, almost senseless, with several marks of violence upon him; in which condition he continued till last Saturday night; and then died, without ever having been able to declare, intelligibly, any particulars of the misfortune which had befallen him. The Coroner's Inquest later sat upon his Body, and brought in their verdict, willful murder against some person or persons unknown.'*

A Notice of Reward gave information that Wynniatt had been robbed of ten pounds, *'the greatest part of which consisted of Portugal pieces contained in an old greasy leather purse.'* The suggestion was that the person (or persons) concerned knew the deceased, *'who has of late carried considerable sums of money about him, and was fond of shewing it in all companies where he was drinking.'* Despite a £50 reward, no information was forthcoming. The subsequent murder, seven months later, of wealthy farmer Stephen Mathews, way-laid and robbed near his home on the Stow road, led to the arrest and execution of Robert Jones, a neighbour of Mathews. Jones was strongly suspected of involvement in Wynniatt's death, but solemnly denied all knowledge to the last.

A most sinister crime was perpetrated in the 1830's by a group termed the Broadway bodysnatchers. It was the practice of these so-called 'resurrectionists' to disinter and sell for medical experiment the corpses of the recently departed. The trade was widespread at the time and very lucrative. A clean corpse could fetch £20 in London, six months wages to an ordinary working man. The remote location of St. Eadburgha's churchyard made it an ideal spot for this group's nocturnal activities. One member of the Broadway gang was 'Nosey' Davies, the son of David Davies, the late curate. Another member was a Whitesmith, whose name is no longer known, who built an ingenious device to remove the coffin lid, and by means of a pulley, lift the body swiftly from the grave. Their activities became public knowledge in 1831, when attempts to sell the body of Mrs. Hannah Ward, a thirty-seven year old pastry cook and wig-maker, went awry. Due to some infection of the leg, which may have been instrumental in her death, the body proved unsaleable, and rather than risk re-interring her, it was unceremoniously dumped in a 'mixen' or muck-heap at the Long

Law, War and Disturbance

Stalls adjoining Church Piece. Days later a terrier was seen scratching on the heap, and after eating its fill, (so the gruesome story is told), ran up Broadway High Street and was never seen again. The following day Mrs. Ward's body was discovered, and identified as such through some peculiarity of the teeth. The resurrectionists, whilst well known, were never caught at their work, but received it is said a kind of natural justice. Of the four gang members, one later shot himself, another left the village and was never heard of again, and the other two died miserably.

One of the most bizarre and extreme political acts to have occurred in the village was the bungled attempt in 1834 to assassinate the Broadway tax collectors. That Broadway was once witness to an act of terrorism may come as a surprise, but the incident underlines the strength of political agitation during the 1830's, the great decade of reform. The paymasters, as they were known, were collectors of revenues such as 'scot and lot,' local taxes often of a trivial kind, which entitled those who had paid them six months prior to a General Election to cast a vote; a right still then denied to the majority. With careful planning, the paymasters were able to pack the register with supporters of their chosen party, often in sufficient numbers to influence the outcome of local contests. For that reason, if no other, they were unpopular in many quarters

In July 1834 the Liberal Prime Minister, Lord Grey, resigned over the use of Irish Church revenues. He was succeeded by his colleague Lord Melbourne. But in November Melbourne's administration was dissolved by William IV, the last time a ministry has been dismissed by a sovereign. Around six o'clock, on the evening of Tuesday 6 December, several paymasters were assembled around a fire in the vestry of the old Chapel in the Snowshill Road; their purpose being doubtless to discuss the forthcoming election. To their astonishment a paper parcel, subsequently revealed to contain gunpowder, suddenly came rattling down the chimney. The device failed to detonate and the 'bombers' disappeared swiftly into the darkness. The next day a hand-bill was issued offering a £50 reward for the discovery of those who *'let fall upon the fire, from the top of the chimney of the chapel, one pound or thereabouts of gunpowder, contained in a paper parcel, with the villainous intent of blowing up and murdering the persons so assembled.'* Thomas Smith, 37, a gardener, and William Jackson, 36, labourer, were brought before the Worcester Epiphany Sessions. But the evidence against them was circumstantial and they were acquitted. The constituency of Worcestershire was won by Liberal candidates Edward Holland of Dumbleton Hall and Thomas Cooke of Bentley, but the

Yew Tree Cottage, High Street, in the 1930's. The Yew tree is thought to be many hundreds of years old.

Conservatives won power under Sir Robert Peel. However, Peel's administration proved short-lived, and Melbourne regained power the following April.

The 1870's witnessed an outbreak in trade union agitation, and of particular relevance to Broadway the formation of the National Agricultural Labourers Union, under its president and founder, Joseph Arch. Broadway contained more than two hundred agricultural labourers, by far the largest group of employed men. It was therefore natural the village should become a focus within the district in the struggle for improved conditions and union recognition.

Agricultural wages had lagged those of industrial workers. But attempts to unionise the labourers proved ill-timed as it coincided with a severe depression in farming. Initially, progress was made in bidding up wages, but farmers were soon able to break the union. In April 1873, at the height of the agitation, Arch visited the village, and after a colourful parade through the streets, banners flying and accompanied by the Broadway Brass Band, he addressed upwards of fifteen hundred villagers from a wagon on the green. In July labourers were addressed by the district committee, but on this occasion the speeches proved less than elevating. Mr. Roberts of

Cropthorne, whose concerns apparently lay with broader political issues, upset spectators by expounding in a 'vulgar style' on the abuses of the police, the magistrates and indeed everyone in authority. Many present drifted away and he ended without a cheer. A meeting in August debated the worrying problem of strangers in the district willing to cut corn below union rates.

In May 1874 a union rally and an anti-union dinner scheduled for the same day created a flurry of excitement in the village. The Anti-Labourers Union Dinner at the Assembly rooms of the Lygon Arms Hotel, was hosted by Mr. J. Wilson Wilson of Austin House. Mr. Wilson Wilson owned several farms, some two dozen farm cottages, and upwards of 600 acres of land in Broadway. In attendance were one hundred and seventy fellow farmers and friends, and a few labourers sympathetic to the cause. The inevitable after-dinner speeches, noteworthy for their rhetorical tone, criticised Arch for his 'vilification' of Her Majesty the Queen, and accused him of going about the country stirring up strife. Mr. Wilson Wilson, acknowledged leader of local opposition to the union, was described by a fellow speaker as the personification of John Bull, a thorough Englishman who, he hoped, would not be imposed upon by the union labourers in his employ. The dinner ended with a plea to the labourers present not to cause trouble with the unionists.

The unionist rally, a somewhat livelier affair, began with a rally in a field loaned by Benjamin Burrows of Lower Mill; support for labourers was by no means confined to the working classes. A noisy procession was then effected through the streets, the sounds of which doubtless reached the ears of those feasting at the Lygon Arms. Accompanied by the Broadway and Alderton Brass Bands, the marchers carried banners stating 'Union is Strength' and 'Arch and Taylor for ever.' After a circuit of the village, they returned to the field where some fifteen hundred unionists, wives, children and supporters, sat down to tea and speeches. Despite their efforts, the labourers won few concessions and farm work remained poorly paid.

Following the dissolution of Disraeli's Conservative administration in 1880, villagers were greatly occupied with the impending General Election and Gladstone's promise to extend the franchise to farm workers. Despite the reform bills of 1832 and 1867, agricultural labourers still had no vote, and were not enfranchised until 1884. In April 1880 the Liberal Party candidates for the constituency of East Worcestershire, W.H. Gladstone, (son of William Ewart Gladstone), and Mr. Hastings visited Broadway. They received an enthusiastic welcome at a meeting in the British Schools room, where Mr. Owen John Morris, of the Upper Mill described Mr. Gladstone as *'a chip off the old block.'*

WORCESTERSHIRE.

PARTICULARS (WITH PLAN)
OF VERY VALUABLE AND ATTRACTIVE
FREEHOLD AND LEASEHOLD
ESTATES

And superior RESIDENCES, situate in the Village and Parish of BROADWAY, in the County of Worcester, being the well-known Properties of JOHN WILSON WILSON, ESQ. The same comprises upwards of

600 ACRES

Of Pasture, productive Aarable, rich Grazing, and choice and extensive Orcharding Land,

And will be offered in suitable Lots as stated in the subjoined particulars, or in such other Lots as may be determined at the time and place of sale.

The Lots include a valuable FARM of 198A. 3R. 35P., Arable and Pasture, with a large and commodious FARM-HOUSE and FARM BUILDINGS, excellently and well arranged, known as the "Top Farm."

A FARM of 37A. 1R. 33P. of first-class Arable and a Field of choice Pasture Ground.

The substantial RESIDENCE called "Springfield," with upwards of 17 Acres of Arable and Pasture Land, of the highest quality, contiguous thereto.

A superior FARM of 50 Acres of Arable and Pasture Land, with convenient Buildings thereon, known as "Masty Farm."

A most valuable ESTATE of 78 Acres of good Arable, Pasture and Orchard Land, known as "The Broadway Hill Farm," with capital FARM-HOUSE and well arranged FARM BUILDINGS.

The Old-established INN known as "The Coach and Horses," with upwards of 14 Acres of choice Pasture Land and most productive Orcharding.

The excellent and well-situated RESIDENCE known as "Cotswold House," with Coach-houses and Stabling attached.

A compact and valuable FARM, comprising 19A. 1R. 13P., called "Owls' Hall," and consisting of sound and excellent Pasture Land, a small portion Orcharding and Coppice.

A singularly attractive and rich GRAZING FARM of 98A. 2R. 7P., called "Pye Corner Farm," with suitable Farm Buildings and Orcharding.

A most charming and convenient RESIDENCE, with Stabling, Outbuildings, and walled-in Garden, the area comprising upwards of One Acre, now occupied by Mr. C. Cook, with a rich Close of Pasture Land, called "Mill Orchard," containing 4A. 3R. 0P.

And the delightfully pleasant, commodious, and well arranged RESIDENCE, known as "Austin House," in the occupation of the Proprietor, with extensive Stabling, Coach-houses and Out-offices, Vinery, Forcing Pits, Pleasure and Kitchen Gardens, and Pasture and Orcharding Lands, containing 48A. 3R. 29P., held with and adjoining the same.

Also 39 ACRES of most fertile, rich and sound Arable, Pasture and Orcharding LAND (in various Lots) called "Pennylands," "Cowley's," "Peasebrook," &c., hereinafter fully described, suitable for Gardening purposes, Building Sites and accommodation holdings.

Together with 25 FARM-HOUSES, COTTAGES or TENEMENTS, with Gardens and convenient Outbuildings attached, lying dispersedly in the Village.

The above will be offered for Sale by Public Auction, by Messrs.

H. W. SMITH & RIGHTON

AT THE LYGON ARMS HOTEL, BROADWAY,
ON THURSDAY, THE 27TH DAY OF JULY, 1876,
At Two o'clock in the Afternoon precisely, by order of the Proprietor, and subject to Conditions of Sale.

Mr. Wilson Wilson sells up. Auction Notice 1876.

Several weeks later a Liberal government was elected, as were Messrs. Gladstone and Hastings who defeated the Conservative candidates Temple and Allsopp. At the news becoming known in Broadway there were noisy scenes of rejoicing. The church bells of St. Eadburgha's were rung, and the Broadway Brass Band made an impromptu appearance playing 'See The Conquering Hero Come,' and other appropriate refrains, at the head of large procession of men, women and children. The Reverend Caffin later apologised for the bells being sounded, for it was done without his knowledge or approval. It was inappropriate, he said, to employ them for a political occasion.

CHAPTER SEVEN

CUSTOM, FOLKLORE AND SUPERSTITION

Folk customs and folklore have enjoyed something of a revival in recent years, although for some villages it has come too late, as many of their largely oral traditions have already been lost. Broadway might have suffered this misfortune were it not for the work of two local men - Christopher French Hensley and John Morris, both students of Broadway's past. In 1924, some twenty years after Hensley's death, Morris published a series of 'Historical Sketches,' in the columns of the *Evesham Journal*. Drawing on his own studies and the work of his late friend, these covered many aspects of village history, in particular its folklore and traditions.

Among the Broadway customs Morris recorded was the practice of spreading corn husks at the door of a wife-beater; the public being thus notified that 'thrashing' had taken place there, and the man hopefully being suitably shamed into mending his ways. Another expression of moral indignation was reserved for unfaithful wives, who could find themselves serenaded in their homes by a mock band of players on pots and pans. Morris recalled an instance of this happening during his lifetime, an effigy of the 'guilty' man also being burnt. It now seems remarkable that such public expressions of moral outrage were ever considered appropriate.

One ancient Broadway custom was embodied in a statute of Henry VII, whereby all who held land in the parish were compelled to pay one penny annually towards the cost of repairing the church, or forfeit twenty pence to the Lord of the Manor. Oak Apple Day (29 May) was celebrated each year at Broadway, as it still is in other parts, to mark the restoration of King Charles II to the throne in 1660. Boys were required to wear an oak apple and a bunch of oak leaves on the day. Those who failed in their duty could find themselves 'captured' by the other boys, who would recite the rhyme,

'The twenty-ninth of May, is Oak Apple Day,' and demand, *'Say, Shik, Shak.'* Those refusing to comply would suffer some schoolboy torture. The traditions associated with the day died out in Broadway around 1870.

There exists a strong tradition of charitable giving in Broadway. A custom of providing loaves of bread to the needy on St. Thomas's Day (21 December) persisted until about 1930. In 1871, the distribution amounted to sixty-eight loaves. Apples and sweets were also given to the children of the village as a sort of Christmas box. The distribution was funded by Knowles' Charity. A Dorcas Society, formed in 1852 of church ladies, provided clothing to the needy, and soup kitchens were a not uncommon feature. During the severe winter of 1880/1 a collection was taken amongst local tradesmen to fund a temporary kitchen which provided five hundred villagers with a cup of soup and a slice of bread several times a week. This was maintained until the weather improved. The British Schools building and Austin House were the usual venues for soup kitchens.

Eighteenth century Manor Court rolls indicate that the country practice of trapping sparrows was indulged at Broadway, the sum of *'2d by the dozen for destroyed sparrows'* being paid. The humble hedgehog, or urchin as it was more commonly known, also attracted the attention of the authorities, carrying the exceptional bounty of 4d. Hedgehogs suffered from the superstition that they stole the milk from cows whilst they rested in the fields, and carried windfall apples away on their backs. Sparrows, doubtless a great pest for the quantity of crops they devoured, were caught in special wicker or wire cages known as sparrow pots. These dome-shaped contraptions had a hole at the top, to allow the bird to enter, and a flange of open-worked wire hanging down inside to prevent escape. It had a bottom like a bird-cage, or was open and stood on a tray where corn or other bait was laid.

Amongst the oldest traditions connected with Broadway was the belief that St. Eadburgha's church once contained a silver peal of bells which were taken down and hidden by the monks at the time of the Dissolution. The burial place was generally believed to be the Court Coppice, a small wood which at one time adjoined the Court in the Bury End, and which today forms part of St. Eadburgha's churchyard. It is not suggested the bells were manufactured entirely of silver. They simply contained an element of the metal, added to give them a sweeter tone. The knowledge that St. Eadburgha's tower is 15th century whilst the earliest bell dates from the 17th century lends some credence to the belief. Other traditions concerned the many ancient tunnels and secret passages reputed to link various houses of the village. However, as no passageways have ever been found, it seems

Custom, Folklore and Superstition

The Proclamation of the Accession of King George V, in front of Croft Villa, by the Village Green. 1911.

Broadway Tower, one of the village's curiosities. Built about 1799 for the Earl of Coventry, on a clear day a reputed thirteen counties are visible.

likely these were mere flights of fancy. Broadway has, for the most part, been a peaceful village, and hardly merited such devious arrangements.

Another tradition holds that, in ancient times, the monks of Pershore Abbey stored fish on the hillside, giving rise to its present name, Fish Hill. However, there is no evidence for this, and indeed it seems likely the name derives from the 18th century coaching Inn called the Fish which, until recent years, stood at the summit. Older documents make no mention of the name, and refer only to the Broadway Hills. It is of course possible that the inn took its name from a legend then current. Early Manor Court rolls point, as we might expect, to the existence of fishponds in Broadway. The 14th century Alburnwell is thought to be an example. Perhaps closer to the legend, a 16th century document refers to a field on the southern slopes called 'Bitteling Hunger;' bitterling of course being a fish, and 'hunger' meaning a place animals were stored prior to slaughter. The modern version of the name is Batten Hangers.

The Fish Inn is mentioned in connection with the sad case of Joseph Dyer, whose brutal murder forms part of local folklore. Dyer was a nurseryman from Chipping Campden who met his end in May 1772, returning from Broadway after journeying there to collect monies owed him. Travelling on foot, he paused on his long journey for a drink at the Inn where he attempted to pay with a 36 shilling piece. The landlord was unable to oblige him with change, but knowing Dyer said he could settle the account when he next called. It is not clear whether his murderer witnessed this transaction, or how otherwise he knew Dyer carried a large sum of money. After finishing his drink, he set out for Campden. But whilst crossing the fields he was set upon from behind and so badly beaten he died there and then. His body was discovered a while later by children out birdsnesting.

Two local men fell under suspicion of the murder and were arrested. But one was quickly released, it being established he had nothing to do with the affair. The other man, William Kealey or Kelly, aged about 22 years, was taken to Gloucester Prison, tried, found guilty and sentenced to hang. As his crime was considered especially wicked, it was judged he should be hanged at the scene of his wrongdoing. On the day of his execution, Friday 2 September 1772, he was transported from Gloucester Prison to Campden Hill, a journey of many hours, in the wagon that also served as his scaffold. Along the route he solemnly protested his innocence, calling God as his witness, but when approaching the murder scene broke down and confessed his guilt. He was joined towards the end of his progress by his mother and sister, and declared to them, and to others gathered to witness the execution, that his crime had been committed on the spur of the moment, and after seeing Dyer lying dead he did not have the heart to rob him. In his speech of contrition to the crowd he attributed his downfall, in part, to the non-observance of the Sabbath, a plea of mitigation that was always welcomed by the presiding priest. Then, as was customary, the hangman handed him an object, in this instance some straw, for him to drop as a signal when he had prepared himself for the hereafter. At three o' clock, before a crowd of several thousand spectators, Kealey made his peace with God and was despatched. His body was hung in chains from a specially constructed gibbet some thirty feet in height so it might be seen from the road. It had been a fine harvest day. But the following week it rained continuously, ruining the crop. This was taken as a judgement on those who had abandoned their work to watch the execution. Both men achieved lasting recognition. The spot where the murder was committed is known as Kealey's Hollow, whilst the road into Chipping Campden from Dovers Hill is called Dyer's Lane.

Of Broadway's many reputed ghosts the most romantic story concerns Anthony Sheldon who fell at the second Battle of Newbury in the Civil War fighting for the King, but 'returned' that night as arranged to rendezvous with his betrothed beneath a tree near St. Eadburgha's church. His ghostly form on a white horse was supposedly seen by a servant thundering down Conigree Lane. The 14th century Priors Manse was said to be haunted by strange noises and the rattling of crockery, and an unusual tradition once held that at midnight there could sometimes be heard the faint sound of a violin. In the abbot's room of Abbots Grange there was occasionally to be witnessed the ghostly figure of a white lady, of unknown provenance, but presumed to be a nun. Another ghostly lady, the unfortunate victim of a hunting accident, was said sometimes to be seen gliding along the hollow into which she fell below Collier's Knap. The old trackway bears the name of White Lady's Walk. An area of open fields opposite Austin House in the Snowshill Road, known as the Wilderness, is thought to be haunted by several ghosts. A fish pond that once existed there, fed by Stonehill Brook, was said to contain the ghost of a certain Nosey Phillipps who, it is alleged, stumbled into the pond one day and drowned. In 1831 William Widdows, whilst attempting to cross the unfenced bridge over Buncher's Brook, fell into the brook and was drowned. He is said thereafter to have haunted the bridge.

The best recorded example of a tragedy, which later gave rise to the suspicion of a ghost, concerns a certain Madame Harpur, an elderly spinster,

The view to the Tower, 1936. (Copyright: Oxfordshire Photographic Archive, DLA, OCC)

The Village Green and High Street, 1930's.

who lived an isolated existence in a mansion that once stood in the Wilderness. The house was reputedly built during the 18th century by the Winnington family, who were then Lords of the Manor. In 1790 the unfortunate Madame Harpur was set-upon by burglars. She died barely a year later never having fully recovered from the experience. Her spirit is said to haunt the hollow by the Waterloo Bridge. The bridge is a later construction, built in 1819 to commemorate Wellington's famous victory, and is reputed to have replaced a more primitive structure. It was said that at the beginning of the 19th century this spot was not crossed after dark without fear or trepidation.

Madame Harpur's ordeal sheds light on some sinister activities of the time. During the winter of 1789 a criminal gang was formed with the intent of robbing houses in the Midlands. In the absence of a police force, organised gangs of this type were among the most feared of criminals. Prominent among its members were William Frazier (or Fraser), described as *'a most hardened man'* and its acknowledged leader, and James Wyllie, a pedlar from Stow-on-the-Wold, whose travels in the area allowed him to identify suitable targets. During December 1789 and January 1790 several burglaries were carried out by the gang. Wyllie then proposed they should rob the home of Madame Harpur at Broadway. The house was known to him as he had visited it many times, and had always been well received by the old

The Wilderness, looking from Bunchers Brook towards Austin House. (Photo: B. Parsons)

lady. The plan was agreed, and a little while later, six or seven members of the gang made their way to Broadway, arriving after nightfall. Wyllie conducted them to the rear of the house where Frazier, the most experienced, broke a pane of glass in the door, turned a key on the inside, and gained admission. To avoid recognition several members of the gang had disguised themselves. Some had blackened their faces. Another had the top of an old stocking over his head with holes cut in it. At least one carried a gun. They seized Madame Harpur's servant and forced her to escort them to her mistress's bedroom, where alarmed by the intruders the old lady cried murder and tried to get to the window. Frazier prevented this, and beat her viciously about the body and head. His confederates later stated that had they not threatened to blow his brains out, Frazier would have set fire to Miss Harpur and burned her in her bed. Their haul for an evil night's work was four coins to the value of about £4.

Several weeks later four members of the gang, including Wyllie and Frazier, were arrested after a robbery at Burton in Warwickshire. Aggravated burglary carried the death penalty, and if convicted they were certain to hang. Frazier, however, anxious to save his own neck, agreed to turn King's Evidence and testify against his former partners. This was only possible because the prosecution lacked the necessary proof against the other gang members. Wyllie was lodged in Worcester Jail for the burglary at Broadway, and at the Spring Assizes his erstwhile partner and Madame Harpur's servant gave evidence for the prosecution. He was found guilty and sentenced to hang. Two weeks later the *Berrows Worcester Journal* reported: *'On Friday last, Wyllie, condemned at our last assizes, was, in pursuance of his sentence, carried in a cart from our castle to the fatal tree; his behaviour there, and on his way thither, seemed to be truly penitent and resigned. He acknowledged the justice of his sentence, and was at twelve o' clock, amidst a numerous concourse of spectators, launched into eternity.'* Frazier was then taken to Warwick where he gave evidence for the prosecution on the burglary at Burton. His companions were condemned and subsequently hanged. To public disgust Frazier was released to resume his criminal activities.

Legend has it that, after robbing Madame Harpur, the villains set fire to the house. There is no indication of this in contemporary reports. But after her death the house fell into decay, and its stone was looted for use in other buildings of the village. The spot where the house once stood became a literal wilderness. Thus an area now designated of 'outstanding natural beauty' had its origins in a brutish crime committed more than two centuries ago.

CHAPTER EIGHT

THE JEWEL OF THE COTSWOLDS

For those who know Broadway, whether as villager or casual visitor, it is quite simply 'the Jewel of the Cotswolds.' To be fair, there are other Cotswold towns and villages that might challenge the use of the title. But perhaps nowhere can there be found a more attractive combination of the natural and man-made. Its houses of honey-coloured stone, of different styles and periods, well-built, supremely individual, yet somehow blending harmoniously with one another. Its rolling countryside and green fields where for at least a dozen centuries crops have been grown and animals grazed. Its quiet backlanes and footpaths, where folk can wander undisturbed. Its broad and busy High Street, the hub of business activity. All form part of the unique character that is Broadway.

Yet the reputation Broadway holds in the public mind is a comparatively recent phenomenon. It is usually credited to the artists and writers for whom Broadway became a favourite haunt in the late 19th century. Ironically, the tranquillity and natural beauty they sought and found was, in part, the result of a once prosperous village brought low through misfortune.

Although Broadway had grown substantially during the early years of the 19th century, the introduction of rail travel in the 1840's caused a severe decline in the passing trade on which it relied. Billings' 1855 Worcester Directory summarised the predicament: *'During the good old coaching days Broadway was a place of considerable note, having been one of the "stages" on the road to Oxford and London, but since the introduction of the "rail" into the country it has lost much of its briskness, and has settled down into a very quiet place, many of its chief inns being closed.'* A Mr. Collett, writing in 1866, remarked on the decline. *'No credible person of small means will come to reside here, and most of the better houses are occupied by almost solitary widows and old maids and bachelors; the farmhouses by labourers or bailiffs.'* An agricultural depression, which began during the 1870's and lasted for several decades, added to the discomfort. A low point for business was reached in 1893 when the tenant of the Lygon Arms Hotel went bankrupt, and its entire contents were put up for auction.

Trade is the lifeblood of Broadway, and the popularising of its charms brought great benefit. From about 1880, although slowly at first, increasing numbers of tourists began to arrive, curious to view this Cotswold gem. Today more than a million visit the village every year. This new phenomenon was initially considered such a novelty that visits were often chronicled in the *Evesham Journal*. In 1894, for example, it was reported there had visited on separate occasions, sixty eight members of the Birmingham Pawnbrokers Association; some sixty students from Cheltenham Ladies College; a party on a field trip from the Cotteswold Naturalists Club; thirty members of the choir of Stratford Congregational Chapel, (who enjoyed an *al fresco* meal on the hill); and a party of employees of Messrs T Bragg, manufacturing jewellers of Birmingham who *'had a stroll around and afterwards met at the Swan Hotel for dinner.'*

J.B.Ball's Grocery Store, High Street, 1931. Now, the Edinburgh Wool Mill.

Gordon Russell Offices, High Street, formerly farm houses. (Photo: B. Parsons)

Whilst visitors today mostly arrive as couples or families, (and in far greater numbers) one might say that little else has changed. The *Birmingham Gazette* in describing the latter visit remarked: *'The famous old village, the delight of artists, especially of Americans, was much enjoyed, the views of the rich and sweeping vales, with the Cotswolds as a background, being varied and brilliant in the sunlight. The quaint buildings of stone, with their grey roofs all variegated with moss and lichen, and so individual in character, were a constant charm...'*

Broadway was then, as perhaps it always has been, a socially mixed community. A newspaper report which described a serious fire at the Lower Mill in 1897 where the entire village appears to have pitched in to help, provides a somewhat humorous insight into the contemporary view of this cultural mix. *'The way in which the various helpers worked,'* it reported, *'was beyond praise, - peer and peasant, artist and artisan, sturdy wives of labourers and delicate ladies vieing with each other as to who should render the most efficient aid.'* At the apex of Broadway society at the turn of the century was Lord Lifford of Austin House; whose memorial hall built in 1915 was an attractive addition to the village. Also prominent were Edgar Flower of Middle Hill and Isaac known to all as Squire Averill of

Broadclose. Little of consequence occurred in the village without their knowledge or involvement. Flower, of the Stratford-upon-Avon brewing family, purchased Middle Hill from the heirs of Sir Thomas Phillipps during the 1880's and restored the house after it had fallen into ruin. Sir Thomas was one of Broadway's most famous sons, a great eccentric and bibliophile of whom many stories are told. A private man who seems not to have involved himself greatly in village affairs, in pursuit of his great stated obsession, - to own a copy of every published work - he filled every room and corridor of his mansion at Middle Hill with his burgeoning collection, much to the discomfort of his family. When he left the village in 1862 to live at Thirlestaine House, Cheltenham, he took with him 133 wagon loads of books and manuscripts. He died in 1872.

The new century brought a revival in Broadway's fortunes, aided by the introduction of the motor car. New men of commerce arrived, attracted by the village's potential. They both witnessed and benefited by Broadway's return to prosperity. The opening of a new railway branch line linking Cheltenham with Birmingham and, via a loop at Honeybourne, with Worcester and Oxford, allowed the masses cheap and easy access to the village. The station opened in 1904 amid much public fanfare, and was finally closed in 1960, since when the line itself has closed and the track has been lifted. Only the large embankment and bridges remain as a reminder.

Among those to recognise Broadway's potential was Sydney Russell, a shrewd businessman, who purchased the Lygon Arms Hotel in 1903. He subsequently restored and extended the Inn, creating one of the most famous country hotels in England. He had three sons. The eldest, Gordon, founded a furniture workshop, originally repairing antiques, but afterwards producing craft furniture. This grew into the internationally renowned office furniture manufacturer Gordon Russell Ltd. It has its office and works in the village and currently employs about one hundred and fifty people. Knighted in 1955, Sir Gordon was a modest man of many achievements, particularly in the field of design.

As Broadway's renaissance brought newcomers to the village, and the population grew, so did the pressure on housing. The result, in the years before the Great War, was the construction of a Council estate on the northern side of the village. The estate was extended during the 1940's and 50's. By the late 1920's, villagers were remarking on how the character of the place had changed in recent years. Whilst larger and more prosperous, it was not without problems. Whilst newcomers were welcomed for the employment they brought, they were often resented for the way they went

An example of the first Council houses, Leamington Road. The development was known locally as the 'White City' as the houses were all whitewashed. (Photo: B. Parsons)

about their business. As the gentrification of Broadway High Street proceeded there were evictions of the cottagers. One prominent hotelier caused grievous scandal by evicting an ex-serviceman, his wife and baby from their cottage. An angry mob besieged his hotel, and when he refused to appear proceeded to break the windows.

After the decline and ultimate disappearance of the manor courts in the early 19th century, village affairs were handled either through the vestry or by the Evesham Rural District Council. The ancient link with Pershore diminished in importance throughout the 19th century, and today is hardly recalled. As Broadway was not a town it had no separate council until the introduction of a Parish Council in 1894. It then acquired limited powers over planning and by-laws. Among the Council's responsibilities was street lighting, and there is much correspondence on the matter in the parish records. Originally the lamps were lit by gas, but electric lighting was introduced for a time when Broadway was connected to the supply in 1928. Coal gas came to the village during the 1870's, and was provided courtesy of the Broadway Gas Company which had its production facility on the Cheltenham Road. The supply was said to be somewhat random, and the

This postcard from the 1930's shows Broadclose House on the right.

smell frequently offensive. The gasometer stood at the rear of premises which were subsequently occupied by Messrs Keen and Stocks' bakery.

Another of the Council's responsibilities was for fire protection. The first volunteer brigade, which contained nine members, was formed in 1895. Until that time Broadway had relied on Evesham, Moreton or Campden for protection. Following the serious fire at Lower Mill in 1897, Edgar Flower purchased a manual fire-engine for the village, and Isaac Averill gifted a plot of land in Keytes Lane for the construction of an engine house. The building has since been replaced by a modern engine house.

Originally, fire-fighting was a communal affair and it was literally a case of 'all hands to the pump.' Cash payments, usually of a few shillings, were made to helpers who, in the case of a protracted fire, were required to man the pump in shifts. This ensured they were never short of volunteers. Firemen were alerted by means of a bell. The original now adorns the library. Later a siren was employed in addition to telegraphic alarms linked to the houses of firemen. Today the firemen, who are still part-time volunteers, carry personal alerters.

The most serious fire this century was the destruction in 1934 of ten workers cottages, the property of Gordon Russell Ltd. The fire made forty-one people homeless, though locals rallied round and a relief fund to compensate them for lost belongings raised over £300. The attractive thatched cottages were not rebuilt, and the land was used to extend the

The Jewel of the Cotswolds

This dramatic photograph shows two of the Gordon Russell cottages ablaze. 1934.

Aftermath of the Gordon Russell fire. 1934.

present Gordon Russell factory. A disastrous fire in 1939 which destroyed the premises of corn merchants Messrs. Titchmarsh & Hunt in the Childswickham Road, highlighted the inadequacy of the fire-fighting equipment. But after the war the service improved by leaps and bounds, and the modern brigade, well-trained and well-equipped, remains a considerable asset to the village.

There has been arguably a greater change to the character of the village during the present century than in any previous one. The most obvious development to the landscape has been the growth in housing on the northern side of the village. Further in-fill development is scheduled once Broadway's much debated by-pass is completed. There is an equally marked change in the composition of villagers, and the patterns of employment. In 1900 a majority earned their living in the village, and perhaps one third of those from agriculture. Today the opportunity for full-time employment is limited and many commute to nearby towns. Farm work has declined and probably employs fewer than fifty. Broadway has become something of a retirement village, and now sees a greater transit of people. In this, it is typical of most modern villages. The sense of community is perhaps not as strong as it once was, and there has inevitably been some loss of amenities in recent years, although the point should not be exaggerated. Broadway's five churches and three schools, its many clubs and associations, attest to its enduring position as one of the most vibrant of all Cotswold villages. And as the new Millenium approaches there is no doubt its future is assured.

****

BIBLIOGRAPHY

Alison R. Ridley and Curtis F. Garfield, The Story of the Lygon Arms, 1992

Amphlett, J. Ed., An Index to Worcestershire Fines 1649-1714, Worcs. Hist. Soc. Jas. Parker & Co, Oxford, 1896

Andrews, Maurice, A Village Remembered, 1971

Baker, A., A Battlefield Atlas of The English Civil War, Ian Allen, 1986

Barnard, E.A.B., Notes & Queries Vol I-III, The Journal Press

Barnard, E.A.B., The Barnard Collection, Evesham Library

Barnard, E.A.B., The Sheldons, Cambridge University Press, 1936

Barratt, Chrichton, Johnston and Marshall Wilson eds., Pershore, A Short History, Ebenezer Baylis & Son Ltd, 1972

Berrows Worcester Journal

Calendar of Patent Rolls, Public Records Office

Cox, B.G., The Vale of Evesham Turnpikes, Tollgates and Milestones, Vale of Evesham Hist. Society, 1980

Evesham Journal and Four Shires Advertiser

Gaut, R.C., A History of Worcestershire Agriculture and Rural Evolution, Worcester Press

Gissing. A., Broadway, A Village of Middle England, J.M.Dent, 1934

Gwilliam W., Worcestershire's Hidden Past, Halfshire Books, 1991

Haines, R.M., Calendar of the Register of Adam de Orleton, Bishop of Worcester 1327-1333, HMSO, 1979

Haines, R.M., The Register of Wolstan de Bransford, Bishop of Worcester 1339-1349, HMSO, 1966

Hatcher, J., Plague, Population and the English Economy, MacMillan Press

Hooke D., Worcestershire Anglo-Saxon Charter Boundaries, The Boydell Press, 1991

Houghton, C.C., A Walk About Broadway, Ian Allen, 1980

Howard, Elizabeth, Lechmere Roll 1275-1280, Worcester County Record Office, Transcribed 1990

J. W. Willis-Bund and Arthur Doubleday eds., Victoria History of the County of Worcester, Constable, 1900

Lee, S. Ed., Dictionary of National Biography, Vol. 36, Smith, Elder & Co., 1893

Marett, Dr. W.P., A Calendar of the Register of Henry Wakefield, Bishop of Worcester 1375-1395, Worcs. Historical Society, 1972

Miller, Rev. G., The Parishes of the Diocese of Worcester, Vol II, Hall & English, 1890

Nash, History of Worcestershire, 1781

Power, E., Medieval English Wool Trade, O.U.P., 1941

Ransome, M., The State of the Bishopric of Worcester 1782-1808, Worcs. Hist. Society, 1968

Sherwood, R., The Civil War in the Midlands 1642-1651, Alan Sutton, 1992

Thorn, F & C., Domesday Book No. 16. Worcestershire, Phillimore, 1982

Thorpe, B. ed., 'Florence of Worcester' Chronicon ex Chronicis, 1848

Trevelyan, G., English Social History, Longman, 1944

WEA Evesham History Workshop, Crime in the Vale of Evesham 1651-1670, Hereford & Worcester County Library, 1987

Whitfield, C., A History of Chipping Campden, Shakespeare Head Press, 1958

Willis-Bund, J.W., Ed., Registrum Sede Vacante 1301-1435, Jas. Parker & Co. Oxford, 1897

Wood, J.V., Some Rural Quakers, Wm. Sessions Ltd. 1991

Wood, M., Domesday - A Search for the Roots of England, BBC Publications

Worcester County Records Archives